IRA
BASICS

the INSTITUTE of financial education
111 EAST WACKER DRIVE/CHICAGO, ILLINOIS 60601

© 1988 by The Institute of Financial Education
Fourth Edition
All rights reserved.
Printed in the United States of America

89012/54321

United States Copyright is not claimed for any material taken from United States Government sources.

No part of this publication may be reproduced, stored in a retrieval system or transmitted, in any form or by any means, electronic, mechanical, photocopying, recording or otherwise without the written permission of the publisher.

The material in this publication was believed to be accurate at the time it was written. Due to the evolving nature of laws and regulations on this subject, The Institute of Financial Education makes no guarantee as to the accuracy or completeness of the information contained in this publication. The material in this book does not purport to be advice. If legal advice or other specialized services and knowledge are required, readers should seek a competent professional. Examples, including names and titles, are purely fictitious and are not intended to represent actual savings institutions nor any real persons, living or dead.

ISBN 0-912857-44-7
Library of Congress Catalog Card Number: 87-82605

Contents

Preface vii

Acknowledgments xiii

Chapter One
Conceptual Framework for IRAs 2

Chapter Two
Eligibility, Contributions and
Deductibility 32

Chapter Three
Distributions 78

Chapter Four
Opening and Servicing IRAs 112

Chapter Five
Simplified Employee Pension Plans 174

Glossary 197

Index 213

Preface

Preface

WITH THE realization that many corporations and private businesses did not offer pension plans and that Social Security retirement benefits were inadequate for many, Congress enacted the Employee Retirement Income Security Act of 1974. This act is commonly referred to as ERISA. One of the main features of the act is the provision that allows for the establishment of Individual Retirement Accounts or IRAs. Since 1974, IRAs have grown in popularity and importance. Most financial institutions now offer IRAs as one of their financial services.

Since 1974, there have been six major tax acts and two technical corrections acts that have affected IRA rules. In addition, the Internal Revenue Service interprets IRA rules in many ways. The IRS issues Treasury regulations, revenue rulings, private letter rulings and other releases that interpret IRA rules as Congress has written them. Furthermore, because IRAs are so popular, many bills are introduced to Congress each year that would change IRA rules.

In times of changing regulations, the need for up-to-date, easily understood materials is critical. In the past, laws and regulations have often been misinterpreted and misunderstood partly due to the unavailability of fundamental information regarding IRAs. Much of the information available today on IRAs is either too technical and narrow in scope or too broad and general to be of practical use to employees who must know and be able to explain the many provisions of IRA law.

IRA Basics was developed with this thought in mind. The purpose of this text is to present a clear and concise overview of the pertinent factors involved in establishing and maintaining IRAs at financial institutions. It is our hope that by exploring the many interrelated aspects of IRAs, this book will provide a general framework that employees can use to enhance their understanding of the legal, regulatory and competitive concerns that are commonly shared by all financial institutions.

The text is divided into five chapters each rich with practical everyday work examples. These chapters address the latest IRA regulations due to the Tax Reform Act of 1986. The first three chapters present basic information about IRAs that employees need to know before talking to customers. Chapter 4 explains how to open an IRA and the necessary administrative duties involved with servicing, record keeping and reporting requirements.

Chapter 5 deals with the establishment and maintenance of several available types of Simplified Employee Pension Plans (SEPs). Explanations of SEPs integrated with Social Security and the recently permitted salary deferral SEPs are provided.

This fourth edition of *IRA Basics* incorporates changes mandated in the Tax Reform Acts of 1984 and 1986 since the last edition was printed. Each user of this text needs to keep abreast of current developments relating to IRA law. Important sources of information include the Internal Revenue Code and regularly published tax reviews. IRA law is continually changing, and it is important that each institution be aware of these changes to better serve its customers.

On a final note, it is hoped that the material in this text will provide its readers with a foundation with which to build a better understanding of IRAs and in the process improve upon an important service offered by financial institutions.

Dale C. Bottom
President
The Institute of Financial Education
January, 1988

Acknowledgments

Instructional Design Department

Edward Rozalewicz
Writer

Ruby Dau-Schmidt
Word Processing Operator

Beverly Johnson
Word Processing Operator

Catherine Scholl
Word Processing Operator

Design and Production Department

Jean Lou Hess
Project Coordinator, Editor

Matthew Doherty
Designer

Michael Tapia
Production Manager

This textbook was developed under the direction of Gail Rafter Meneley, Vice President of Marketing, and John Schmidt, AIA, Vice President of Operations.

Institute textbooks are created under the guidance of two department directors: Naomi W. Peralta, Instructional Design, and Robert W. Brown, Design and Production.

The Institute thanks the following individuals who provided assistance and reviewed portions of the manuscript:

Vito C. DeFrisco, Assistant Vice President and Branch Manager, Bell Federal Savings, Chicago, Illinois

Mark Kareken, Attorney, Universal Pensions, Inc., Brainerd, Minnesota

Daniel A. Notto, Vice President and General Counsel, Universal Pensions, Inc., Brainerd, Minnesota

Evelyn G. Swanson, Oak Park, Illinois

Janet R. Wells, Regional Vice President, First Nationwide Bank, Chesterfield, Missouri

Also, The Institute appreciates the cooperation of:

Tom Toft and Lillie Johnson, SAF Systems and Forms

IRA Basics

Conceptual Framework for IRAs

Chapter One

Chapter One
Objectives

After studying this chapter, you should be able to:
- Define and give examples of vesting and portability;
- Identify the three retirement savings programs created under ERISA;
- Explain two tax benefits of an IRA;
- Describe the eligibility requirements for IRAs;
- Differentiate among the five types of IRA contributions; and
- Identify five IRS tax penalties an IRA participant would incur for various actions.

Because consumers increasingly are realizing that they must plan for retirement, they are establishing retirement savings plans at earlier ages than in the past. More and more people are realizing that Social Security alone cannot cover the expenses of a desirable lifestyle. Consumers are becoming increasingly better educated about the need for retirement planning and the available retirement options that could provide them with supplemental income.

Consumers trust financial institutions to help them meet their retirement savings needs. To warrant this trust, employees in financial institutions should be knowledgeable about competitive retirement plans that are available to consumers. They should understand the types of investment vehicles their own institutions offer, as well as alternative investment opportunities available elsewhere. To help consumers plan appropriately, employees should be aware of other sources of retirement income that consumers may have. Also, to help consumers effectively meet their retirement goals, employees should remind them to consider other important factors such as the following:
- Where will they live?
- Do they have adequate medical insurance?
- Have they periodically reviewed their wills?
- Have they established an estate plan to minimize taxes?

Although savings counselors cannot give legal, medical or tax advice to their customers, they can encourage customers to seek these services from other professionals in order to complete their retirement plans. However, the financial institution employee should be able to explain to the customer how the institution's available products can be used in a retirement savings plan and the advantages of doing so.

The main advantage of a retirement savings plan is the opportunity to earn and to keep extra funds. Because certain retirement savings plans enjoy preferential tax treatment, money that is put into them compounds, or grows faster than money invested in identical investments outside of qualified plans. In qualified plans, earnings are tax-deferred; income taxes are postponed on any gains until the funds are withdrawn. Since no taxes are initially paid on the earnings, the entire gain can be reinvested to grow faster than if a portion of the earnings must be used to pay taxes. In addition, individuals' contributions may be partially or wholly deductible on their income tax returns, producing further savings.

Although Congress and the Internal Revenue Service permit individuals to establish IRAs that allow retirement savings to grow tax-deferred, IRA rules must be followed in order to enjoy this preferential tax treatment. This chapter introduces some basic terms, describes who may open an IRA and differentiates among the five types of IRA contributions. Later chapters provide a more detailed study of the legal requirements of retirement plans.

Pension Plan Concept

A *pension plan* is a system that employers and employees establish and maintain so that they can continue to receive an income after they retire. Usually, these plans require employees to be a minimum age and have completed a minimum period of employment to be eligible to participate. For example, being 21 years of age and having one year of service are the common age and length-of-service requirements for pension plan participation. *Participation* is the term used to describe the fact that an employee has joined a pension plan. During the employee's participation, the employer makes payments, known as *contributions*, to the plan. In fact, employers' contributions typically represent the majority of the funds paid into pension plans. Many pension plans permit employees to make a nominal contribution, too. However, most plans are totally supported by employers' contributions and, therefore, require no employee contributions. In either case, contributions become *accrued benefits*, meaning that they may gain in value over time as the plan's administrators invest the pension funds.

After a certain period of time, the employer's contributions to the plan become vested. *Vesting* means that the employee's rights to benefits will not be lost, regardless of whether or not the employee continues to work for that employer. Thus, vested benefits are said to be *nonforfeitable benefits*. Each pension plan uses its own formula to determine how much vesting will occur at set intervals during an employee's participation. In some plans, the employee's accrued benefits are vested in increments according to a progressive schedule, resulting in full vesting after the required period of participation (see Figure 1-1). Other plans use an all-or-nothing system in which the employee's accrued benefits are never partly vested. Instead, full vesting occurs after the required period of participation, but no benefits are vested prior to full vesting (see Figure 1-2). In contrast to other pension plans, there are no vesting provisions for IRAs. All contributions and accrued earnings in an IRA immediately are nonforfeitable.

Regardless of a plan's vesting formula, accrued benefits must in fact be vested—either in part or in full—for the employee to enjoy a nonforfeitable right to these funds. For example, suppose that Mike Lynch leaves his employer after four years of service. If the employer uses a five-year full vesting schedule like the one shown in Figure 1-2, Mike is not entitled to any benefits. However, if Mike leaves his employer after five years of employment, he will eventually receive his full share of the accrued benefits because they are fully vested. By comparison if the employer uses a graded or progressive vesting schedule like the one shown in Figure 1-1, Mike is entitled to 40% of his accumulated retirement benefits after four years of service. Mike is said to be 40% vested. Depending on the type of plan, vested benefits are

FIGURE 1-1
Example of Seven-Year Graded Vesting

Years of Employment	Percent Vested
1 through 2	0%
3	20%
4	40%
5	60%
6	80%
7 or more	100%

received at termination or deferred until retirement.

The Internal Revenue Service rules on whether or not a submitted plan can become a qualified plan.[1] The term *qualified plan* refers only to the special tax classification granted by the Internal Revenue Service. Qualification is not a requirement of a plan but is rather a process of insuring that the retirement plan is written both correctly in terms of the law—particularly Section 401 of the Internal Revenue Code—and equitably in terms of its provisions. In addition to pension plans, qualified plans include profit-sharing, stock bonus, annuity, bond purchase and tax-sheltered annuity plans.

Only if a plan has been qualified can income earned by the plan's investments be temporarily tax-sheltered. *Tax-sheltering* is a legal means of postponing or reducing the tax liability—in this case, on federal income taxes. The tax is deferred until the employee retires and receives either *distributions* (periodic payments from the plan's benefits) or a *lump-sum distribution* (a single payment of the plan's benefits) under certain circumstances.

Pension plans that allow employee contributions in addition to employer contributions are called *contributory plans*. Under contributory plans, several funds are created. One fund is for employer contributions, on which income taxes are being deferred until retirement. Employee contributions can be made into either one or two separate funds depending on whether income taxes on the employee's contributions are being deferred (called *pretax*) or have already been paid (called *after tax*). This multifund approach is used whether or not the plan is "qualified."

FIGURE 1-2
Example of Five-Year Full Vesting

Years of Employment	Percent Vested
1 through 4	0%
5	100%

Major Retirement Plan Legislation

The federal government has long taken an active role in protecting employees' rights and interests in pension plans. Assuring equitable tax treatment has been one of the foremost legislative concerns. In 1926, the government exempted from federal income tax all pension trusts created by employers for the exclusive benefit of employees. In 1928, employer contributions to such exempt trusts were made a deductible business expense. The 1942 Internal Revenue Code stated that pension plans could qualify for favorable tax treatment, provided that they met certain requirements.

In 1962, Congress approved the Self-Employed Individuals Tax Retirement Act, commonly known as the Keogh Act. This act permits certain self-employed persons to set aside a portion of their income in a tax-sheltered retirement plan, known as a *Keogh plan*. Among those who may establish Keogh plans are owners of nonincorporated businesses, sole proprietors, partners and all persons who have income earned from self-employment.

A Keogh plan is tax-sheltered. The funds contributed to the retirement plan by the participant are not taxed; they are deducted from the participant's taxable income. Also, interest earned on these funds is tax-deferred. At retirement, when Keogh plan funds are paid out, income taxes become due. However, at retirement an individual typically will be in a lower tax bracket, which results in a lower tax on the Keogh funds as they are received.

ERISA and Pension Reform

The goal of pension reform has been twofold: to insure financial independence for the retirement years and to equalize the opportunity to participate in a pension plan.

A major step in revising pension regulations was ERISA, the Employee Retirement Income Security Act of 1974 (also known as the Pension Reform Act). ERISA addressed three basic concerns:
- reform of private industrial pensions;
- changes in Keogh plans; and
- creation of the Individual Retirement Savings Program, of which IRA is a part.

To achieve these basic concerns and to protect the interests of pension plan participants, ERISA:
- set minimum standards for participation, vesting and funding;
- required employers to provide plan termination insurance; and
- required certain conduct by the plan's administrators, including disclosure of information to the federal government and to participants.

ERISA also amended the Internal Revenue Code to provide for three tax-deferred individual retirement savings programs: deposit accounts or IRAs, retirement annuities and retirement bonds. In a broad sense, all of these plans often are referred to as IRAs because the tax laws on eligibility, contributions and distributions apply equally to all three.

Today, only IRAs and retirement annuities are still being opened; however, some retirement bonds may still exist. The Treasury stopped accepting applications for U.S. Retirement Bonds on May 1, 1982. U.S. Retirement Bonds that were issued earlier and that are still outstanding will continue to bear interest until the earlier of the date the registered owner reaches 70½ or five years after the registered owner dies, but no later than the date he or she would have reached 70½ if he or she had lived. Retirement bonds may be redeemed before age 59½ and rolled over tax free.

Under the original guidelines of ERISA, to participate in a contributory IRA, an individual must not have been, at any time during the year, an active participant in a qualified pension plan. The same definition of an active participant that previously prevented an individual from *opening* an IRA now *restricts* an IRA participant's *deductibility* of his or her contribution. Specifically, ERISA disqualified from IRA participation any individual who was an active participant in:
- an Internal Revenue Code Section 401(a) qualified retirement plan (a corporate pension plan or a Keogh plan);
- a profit-sharing plan;
- a government pension plan;
- a qualified bond purchase program; or
- a special annuity established for employees of tax-exempt organizations.

Today, an individual who is an active participant in

any of the above-mentioned plans may contribute into an IRA. However, individuals above certain income levels face restrictions on their available tax deductions for contributions.

Other Retirement Legislation

Since their inception, retirement plans have grown both in size and popularity. Because of their increasing importance, tax laws that govern their existence are continuously changing. Some of the more significant legislation that has affected retirement plans is briefly explained below.

Two important IRA changes were the result of the Tax Reform Act of 1976. One increased contribution limits for IRAs and the second permitted wage earners to establish tax-sheltered retirement benefits for their nonworking spouses, known as spousal IRAs. The contribution limits for spousal IRAs were set slightly higher than the limits for contributory IRAs, provided certain regulations are met.

Another important legislative action that expanded the types of IRAs available was the Revenue Act of 1978. Under this act, simplified employee pension plans (SEPs) were created. With SEPs, an employee establishes and maintains an IRA to which employer contributions are made.

SEPs make it easy for small business employers to offer their employees retirement benefits. Like qualified plans, benefits under a SEP must be provided for all eligible employees. However, because SEPs use the same documents, administration and reporting requirements that IRAs do, they are much easier for everyone involved to understand. Another advantage of SEPs is that the contributory limits are higher than those for contributory IRAs.

In 1981, Congress passed the Economic Recovery Tax Act of 1981. This Act greatly expanded IRA eligibility and increased the contribution limits for IRAs and Keogh plans, effective for the 1982 taxable year.

In 1982, the Tax Equity and Fiscal Responsibility Act (TEFRA) was passed. This act had three major effects on pension plans:
- It increased contribution limits for Keogh plans.
- It allowed Keogh plan holders to act as trustees of their own accounts.
- New qualification requirements for certain key employees were adopted for corporate and non-corporate pension plans.

The Tax Reform Acts of 1984 and 1986 further fine-tuned the rules on retirement plans. Since these are the most current acts affecting IRAs and qualified plans, they are covered in detail as they apply to specific topics throughout this text.

A short summary of the federal government's ongoing support for retirement savings plans is shown in Figure 1-3. It illustrates that the scope of eligibility and the increased contribution amounts that qualify for tax shelter have increased greatly since the original Keogh Act in 1962.

The legislation enacted in support of retirement programs is contained in the Internal Revenue Code, which is the major reference source for laws regarding the tax status, reporting and tax liability of IRAs. In addition to the Code, the supervisory agencies for the different types of financial institutions have drafted specific rules concerning open-

FIGURE 1-3
Major Retirement Savings Plan Legislation

Legislation	Major Provisions
Keogh Act of 1962	■ Created Keogh plans—tax sheltered retirement savings plans for self-employed.
Employee Retirement Security Act of 1974 (ERISA)	■ Authorized the Individual Retirement Income Savings Program which established IRAs (deposit accounts), retirement annuities and retirement bonds to which regular or rollover contributions could be made. ■ Liberalized Keogh plans.
Tax Reform Act of 1976	■ Increased allowable contributions for IRAs. ■ Created spousal IRAs.
Revenue Act of 1978	■ Created Simplified Employee Pension Plans.
Economic Recovery Tax Act of 1981	■ Increased allowable contributions for IRAs and Keoghs. ■ Expanded IRA eligibility to employees covered under qualified plans. ■ Eased the contribution restrictions for spousal IRAs.
Tax Equity and Fiscal Responsibility Act of 1982	■ Increased allowable contributions for Keoghs. ■ Eased limits on additional and voluntary contributions. ■ Permitted Keogh plan holders to act as trustees of their own accounts. ■ Created new qualification requirements for top-heavy retirement plans.*
Tax Reform Act of 1984	■ Expanded the rules that apply to lump-sum or plan termination distributions from qualified plans to rollovers. ■ Eased the time limitations for taking distributions from IRAs and Keoghs.
Tax Reform Act of 1986	■ Kept IRA eligibility open to all workers, but restricted ability to deduct contributions for people defined as "active participants" in qualified plans. ■ Shortened minimum vesting schedules for employees. ■ Expanded qualified plan rules that protect employees from discrimination.

*A top-heavy retirement plan, corporate or noncorporate, pertains to those plans where account balances or accumulated benefits for key employees exceed 60% of such amounts for all participants.

ing and maintaining retirement accounts in such areas as disclosure, permissible funding methods, interest rates and withdrawal penalties.

Who Can Contribute

For most types of IRAs, an individual must meet two requirements to become eligible to make contributions. These requirements concern age and compensation (see Figure 1-4). The exceptions to the following age and compensation requirements pertain to spousal IRAs, SEPs and IRAs into which rollovers are made. These types of IRAs are covered later in this chapter.

Age

IRAs are intended to be retirement savings programs rather than tax-sheltered, estate-building devices. For this reason a maximum age

---

FIGURE 1-4
IRA Eligibility Requirements

Age	A participant cannot contribute for or after the taxable year in which age 70½ is reached (except for spousal, rollover and SEP contributions).
Compensation	A participant must have earned income such as: ■ salaries ■ wages ■ professional fees ■ commissions ■ tips ■ bonuses

requirement was established. An individual cannot establish or contribute to either regular or third-party sponsored IRAs for or after the taxable year in which he or she reaches the age of 70½. This maximum age requirement holds even if the individual is still employed at this age. However, there is no minimum age requirement for eligibility.

There are three exceptions to the age 70½ restriction:
- Spousal IRA contributions may be made by a working spouse who is over 70½ if those contributions are made on behalf of a spouse not yet 70½.
- SEP contributions must be made for all eligible employees, including those over age 70½.
- Rollover contributions can be made at any age.

These exceptions are explained in more detail in Chapter 2.

Compensation

For most types of IRAs, a participant's allowable contribution is determined only by the amount of earned income or compensation received, not the participant's total income. *Compensation* is defined as salaries, wages, professional fees and other payments received for personal services actually rendered—such as a salesman's commissions, compensation based upon a percentage of profits, commissions on insurance premiums, tips and bonuses. Compensation includes income earned from self-employment in which the individual's personal services are a material income-producing factor for that trade or business. Compensation also includes alimony received.

Compensation, however, does not include passive

income such as earnings from investments (such as stock dividends), interest from deposit accounts, or rents from buildings or real estate. Income accrued by persons in a partnership who have a financial interest but not a working interest, i.e., silent partners, is not considered compensation. This is an important point that eludes many IRA participants who do not distinguish between income and compensation. The IRA law, however, does make this distinction. Therefore, an IRA participant who earns $1,000 in salary and $5,000 from various investments over the taxable year has earned $1,000 in compensation—the $5,000 in investment income cannot be used as a basis for calculating the individual's contribution limit.

Deductibility of IRA Contributions

Although anyone who meets the age and compensation eligibility requirements may establish and contribute to an IRA, the Internal Revenue Code Section 219(g) is amended by the Tax Reform Act of 1986 Section 1101(a) to restrict the deductibility of IRA contributions. Under the Tax Reform Act of 1986, the deductibility of an IRA contribution is affected, for tax years after 1986, if an IRA participant is also an active participant in an employer-sponsored qualified plan and his or her adjusted gross income is above a specified amount. *Adjusted gross income* is total income minus allowable adjustments to income for tax purposes. Deductibility will not be affected if:
- the individual is single and has an adjusted gross income of $25,000 or less;
- a married couple, filing jointly, has an adjusted gross income of $40,000 or less; or
- the married individual who is covered by a plan files singly and has an adjusted gross income of $0.

If the adjusted gross income exceeds the above limits, the IRA deduction (but not the ability to contribute) will either be reduced or eliminated depending on the dollar amount of the individual's or couple's adjusted gross income. Determining the actual amount an individual or couple may deduct is covered in greater detail in a later chapter.

Types of IRA Contributions

There are five types of IRA contributions: contributory or regular; spousal; third-party, sponsored by an employer, a union or an employee association; simplified employee pension plans (SEPs), funded by contributions to employees' IRAs; and rollover contributions to IRAs.

Contributory

A *contributory* or *regular IRA* is one opened by an employed individual. The individual, called the IRA participant, may contribute compensation up to the limits established for each taxable year.

Spousal

A *spousal IRA* is a special kind of IRA contribution created by the Tax Reform Act of 1976. This legislation permits a working spouse to contribute to an IRA established for his or her nonworking spouse. The Tax Reform Act of 1986 also permits a couple to elect to designate a contribution as spousal even if both spouses have compensation. This change is effective for the 1986 tax year. A financial institution must handle spousal IRA contributions by opening a separate account for each spouse. This is necessary because the law does not permit IRA accounts to be jointly owned.

In effect, the contribution rather than the account has the "regular" or "spousal" character, and this can change from one year to the next. For instance, Samuel and Sadie Johnson establish a spousal IRA with Samuel's compensation; Sadie is not employed. The following year Sadie takes a part-time job and decides to make regular IRA contributions of her own. Her regular IRA contributions may be made to her spousal account. In effect, the spousal IRA is then converted into a contributory account.

Third-Party Sponsored

Employers and employee associations, including unions, can establish and make contributions to IRAs on behalf of their employees under the rules for *third-party sponsored IRAs*. Third-party contributions can also be made to a nonworking spouse's account. The maximum allowable contribution to third-party sponsored IRAs is the same as for contributory IRAs.

In establishing a third-party sponsored IRA, the third party—typically an employer—usually executes an agreement that has been submitted for approval to the Internal Revenue Service. The assets in this type of IRA program may be held in a common fund, but each participant's funds must be accounted for separately. A common practice is to establish a separate account for each participant.

The sponsor is free to be selective in deciding which employees are to be admitted into the IRA program. For example, an employer may decide to establish IRAs only for management personnel.

Similarly, a union or an employee association may choose to establish IRAs only for employees in good standing who have met certain qualifying standards.

Amounts contributed to these IRAs are considered to be part of the employee's compensation. Thus, third-party sponsored contributions are subject both to Social Security (FICA) taxes paid by the employer and the employee and to federal unemployment taxes paid by the employer. However, these IRA contributions are not subject to federal withholding taxes. Contributions to third-party sponsored IRAs can also be made as voluntary payroll deductions from after-tax income. All institutions that have the authority to offer contributory IRAs also can offer third-party sponsored IRAs.

Simplified Employee Pension Plan

The Revenue Act of 1978 created a new and different type of IRA termed a *simplified employee pension plan* (SEP). A SEP is an IRA that is funded by an employer's contributions to employees' IRAs. This new program is totally distinct and separate from third-party sponsored IRAs or any other preexisting types of IRAs under IRA law. The maximum contribution limits are higher than the limits for any other type of IRA. In addition to the employer's contribution to the SEP, employees can contribute to an IRA subject to the same maximum limits established for IRAs.

Under this plan, employers contribute up to an established dollar limit or percentage of earned income. However, employers must establish a written allocation formula under which contributions to employees' IRAs are determined. Such a formula must reflect the particular nondiscrimination and eligibility requirements that apply to the program. Within certain guidelines, employers must apply the requirements uniformly to employees who will be covered by the plan.

Rollovers vs. Transfers

Rollover contributions were first created by ERISA to encourage the development of savings programs. A *rollover* is a distribution from a qualified plan or IRA to the participant, who subsequently reinvests all or part of the distribution in an IRA. Rollover provisions allow for an uninterrupted tax shelter for the proceeds of a qualified pension plan that are received by an employee due to retirement, separation from a company or termination of a plan. Rollover contributions allow an employee who leaves an employer and receives a lump-sum distribution, or an employee who receives a distribution because of plan termination, to deposit all or any portion of this distribution into an IRA. The transfer of rights from one pension plan, or from one IRA, to another plan or IRA is termed *portability*. By taking advantage of portability, employees can continue to build accumulated and vested retirement savings. In addition, the lump-sum distribution, which normally would be considered ordinary income, is tax-sheltered to the extent it is deposited as a rollover contribution.

Rollover transactions were created to provide a continuous tax shelter for retirement funds. All financial institutions with the authority to accept regular contributory IRA contributions also have the authority to accept rollover contributions.

Rollover transactions are different from IRA transfers. The Internal Revenue Service has ruled that a transfer of an IRA directly from one trustee to another is not a rollover and is therefore not subject to the rules and regulations governing rollovers. For example, if Fourth Savings directly transfers Russell Smith's IRA to First Metro Bank, the transaction is considered an IRA-trustee-to-IRA-trustee transfer.

On the other hand, if Russell asks Fourth Savings to give him the funds from his IRA so that he may transfer the funds himself to First Metro Bank, this transaction is a rollover. Thus, IRA transfers are direct transactions between institutions serving as trustees. However, rollovers involve a distribution of the IRA funds to the IRA participant in the participant's name and his or her subsequent establishment of another IRA with the funds.

In general, rollovers can be used in three ways. First, an individual participating in any retirement savings plan—whether it is an IRA, an annuity or a bond—can roll over the funds to another retirement savings plan. For example, if higher interest rates are being paid for an IRA, the holder of retirement bonds can roll over all or any portion of the funds into the IRA. However, an IRA sponsor, or trustee, may impose a penalty on the participant for withdrawing funds from an account before its maturity.

Second, an individual can roll over funds from an employee's qualified pension plan to an IRA. In this case, to qualify for a rollover, the individual must either leave the employer and receive a distribution from the plan or receive a distribution because the employer's plan was terminated. After receiving a partial or total distribution from the plan, the individual can roll over all or any portion of the funds into an IRA. By making a rollover contribution, the individual's retirement funds can be invested for additional growth while enjoying the tax-deferred benefits of IRA participation.

Third, a rollover contribution can be used as a conduit. A *conduit IRA* is a type of IRA established with a rollover contribution for the temporary purpose of holding retirement funds being transferred from one retirement plan to another. An individual who wants to transfer retirement funds from one qualified pension plan to another uses a conduit IRA as a temporary shelter for the funds. Conduits specifically address the problem of pension portability.

Typically, qualified pension plans require a certain waiting period before a new employee is eligible to participate. While an employee waits to enter a new pension plan, the former plan's funds can be protected from taxation as income by being rolled over into a conduit IRA until they can be placed under the new employer's plan. The law does not permit an IRA that originated as a contributory IRA to be converted into a conduit. Thus, "original" IRA funds cannot be rolled over from the IRA to a qualified plan. Also, once a rollover of qualified plan funds is put in the same IRA that holds regular contributions that IRA no longer can be used as a conduit.

In all three instances, funds used to make a rollover contribution to an IRA are subject to particular rules and regulations that are covered in a later chapter. The law currently permits participants to use IRA-to-IRA rollovers once each 12 months, beginning on the date the funds are distributed from the first IRA for rollover purposes.

Under certain conditions, noncash property such

as stocks or other securities can be sold by individuals and the proceeds used to establish rollover IRAs. Similarly, financial institutions may, within specific limitations, accept and convert noncash property for rollover contributions.

Advantages of IRAs

If all the legal requirements established for an IRA are met, earnings grow faster than the same investment outside an IRA could. This faster growth is accomplished because IRA earnings are tax-deferred, allowing all earnings to be reinvested. An IRA participant can begin to withdraw, or take distributions without penalty, from the IRA as early as age 59½ or wait until age 70½. Because IRA participants will usually wait until retirement before taking their distributions, they are likely to be in a lower tax bracket than when they were working. Also, only amounts withdrawn become taxable while the remaining funds in the IRA continue to grow tax-deferred. In addition to deferring taxes on all earnings, participants may be eligible to deduct either all or a part of their annual contributions from their federal income taxes. Some states also allow deductions for IRA contributions from state income taxes.

Disadvantages of IRAs

The advantages of establishing and contributing to an IRA, regardless of whether contributions are deductible, far outweigh the disadvantages of following the laws and restrictions, such as those pertaining to who is eligible to contribute, the age when contributions are no longer permitted and time restrictions as to when IRA funds may be withdrawn. If the IRA participant complies with these restrictions, his or her contributions will grow faster than the same investments made outside of an IRA. However, if laws are not followed, the IRS will impose tax penalties.

Restrictions

Laws discourage individuals from using IRAs as short-term, tax-deferred investment vehicles to be withdrawn whenever a participant wishes. Because IRAs are intended to provide retirement income, before contributions are made participants should determine that their contributions will not be needed before age 59½, or retirement. A major disadvantage of this restriction is that future income expectations and needs before retirement are not easy to predict. The tax consequences of withdrawing too early may be higher tax liabilities and a lower total return than if the participant had invested outside of an IRA. This adverse consequence becomes less severe the longer the contribution remains in the IRA because the gains received from tax-deferred growth will eventually be greater than the tax consequences of early withdrawal.

IRA Penalties

The three types of retirement plans—retirement savings accounts, retirement annuities and retirement bonds—were specifically created by ERISA to help foster retirement savings. Congress has enacted penalties to discourage the use of IRAs for other purposes. These penalties, which are detailed in sections of the Internal Revenue Code, fall into two general categories: loss of tax shelter and specific tax penalties. There are five specific IRS-imposed tax penalties.

Loss of Tax Shelter
Certain conduct on the part of the IRA participant and/or the holder of the IRA funds may cause the loss, either in part or in whole, of an IRA's tax shelter. In most circumstances, only a specific portion of an IRA will be subject to such tax-shelter loss. Should the Internal Revenue Service disqualify (declare ineligible for favorable IRA tax treatment) funds in or distributed from an IRA, the amount disqualified is then included in the participant's taxable income for the year in which the distribution or disqualifying act occurred. Thus, the disqualification of an IRA could entail a heavy tax burden.

IRA funds may be disqualified due to various specific, technical prohibitions. For example, IRA participants are not allowed to pledge or use the IRA funds as collateral for a loan. However, circumstances involving disqualification of the entire IRA are very rarely encountered for IRAs established at financial institutions.

Under particular conditions, the Internal Revenue Service may impose specific tax penalties on the IRA participant in addition to subjecting the amount involved to income taxation. Holders of IRA funds, such as financial institutions, are not penalized in terms of their tax liabilities.

Specific Tax Penalties
Certain types of prohibited conduct may lead to the imposition of specific tax penalties by the Internal Revenue Service. There are currently five specific tax penalties. These specific penalties are in addition to any regular income tax due plus any

loss of interest penalties imposed by the institution, such as in the case of the early withdrawal of funds from certificates of deposit. These tax penalties are expressed routinely as percentages of the amount at issue.

In general, specific tax penalties relate to conduct concerning both the timing and the amounts of contributions and distributions. Some examples are the following:

- A 6% excess contribution penalty.

  If an IRA participant's contributions exceed the particular limitations for that account, a 6% penalty may be imposed upon the excess.

- A 10% early distribution penalty.

  If a distribution is made before age 59½ for any reason besides those permitted (these will be covered in a later chapter), a 10% penalty is imposed.

- A 50% underdistribution penalty.

  If, after age 70½, the minimum required distribution is not taken, then a 50% penalty is imposed on the amount that should have been withdrawn but was not.

- A 15% excess distribution penalty.

  A 15% IRS penalty tax will be imposed on certain types of distributions made after December 31, 1986, that, in the aggregate, exceed $112,500 during any calendar year. The $112,500 figure is to be indexed at the same time and in the same manner as the dollar limitation on annual benefits under a defined benefit pension plan. This penalty does not apply to distributions over the $112,500 figure pertaining to amounts distributed due to death, a qualified domestic relations order, distributions of nontaxable contributions or amounts that are rolled over within 60 days of distribution.

- A 15% excess retirement accumulation tax.
  This penalty is an additional, one-time federal estate tax that is paid by the individual's estate at the time of death if an individual's balance in all retirement plans is too large. If at the time of death an individual's interests in qualified retirement plans, tax-sheltered annuities and IRAs exceed the present value of an annuity with annual payments of $112,500 (or the limitation in effect), an excess retirement accumulation results. The annuity value is calculated by using the individual's life expectancy just before death. For example, if the deceased lived to age 66, then the annuity value used would be the life expectancy of a 66-year-old. The 15% excess retirement accumulation tax is levied against the amount of the present value of the annual annuity payments that exceed $112,500. This is a one-time tax paid by the individual's estate. For example, if a participant with a life expectancy of 10 years dies leaving account balances that would purchase a 10-year annuity of $132,500, the penalty estate tax would be $3,000—15% on the excess, or [($132,500 - 112,500) X .15].

Summary

The proportion of older Americans to the total population is projected to increase throughout the coming decades. Thus, retirement planning options are becoming a more serious issue.

Under a pension plan, an employer can provide retirement benefits for employees. An employee who is an active participant in a pension plan obtains certain rights, often after a specified period of employment with one employer. Once the accumulated benefits of the employee become vested, they are nonforfeitable, regardless of whether or not the employee continues to work for the employer.

The Keogh Act passed in 1962 created a tax-sheltered retirement plan for self-employed persons. ERISA established the first retirement savings plans for individuals—IRAs. Rollover contributions to IRAs were developed to provide uninterrupted tax-sheltering for an employee's benefits from a qualified pension plan. Conduit IRAs allow the transfer (portability) of vested benefits from one qualified plan to another. In 1976, spousal contributions to IRAs were first authorized to allow deductible contributions to be made to an IRA for a nonworking spouse. Small business employers are permitted to contribute to IRAs established by their employees through a SEP.

In general, the eligibility requirements for most types of IRAs specify that to contribute to an IRA, an individual must receive earned income or compensation. In addition, an individual may not contribute for the tax years during or after attaining age 70½. However, an individual may make rollover or SEP contributions after age 70½. Compensation includes salaries, wages, commissions, tips and bonuses but does not include earnings from interest or rental fees. An individual who is an active participant in a qualified pension plan is not restricted from establishing or contributing to an IRA, but may have his or her ability to deduct the contribution curtailed.

Individuals who want to contribute to regular or spousal IRAs or who receive third-party sponsored IRA contributions must meet the age and compensation requirements. For spousal IRA participants, both spouses may now earn compensation during the taxable year.

An individual is eligible to make a rollover contribution to an IRA upon receiving a total or partial distribution from a qualified plan at age 59½ or upon leaving the employer. All or any portion of the distribution may be contributed to an IRA.

SEP participants, as well as Keogh plan and third-party sponsored IRA participants, are allowed also to establish and contribute to their own contributory IRAs.

Taxes on retirement savings are deferred in two ways. First, amounts contributed may be able to be deducted from gross income. Second, IRA contributions and interest earned are tax-deferred until withdrawals are made at retirement. To discourage a participant from using IRA funds for purposes other than retirement savings, the Internal Revenue Code imposes penalties, such as a loss of tax shelter or the imposition of a specific, percentage-based penalty tax.

Chapter Questions

1. Explain with examples the terms *vesting* and *portability*.
2. Name the three retirement savings programs that ERISA created.
3. What are the two major tax benefits of an IRA?
4. What are the age and income requirements to be eligible to establish an IRA?
5. Define and give an example of each of the following types of IRA contributions: contributory, spousal, third-party sponsored, SEP and rollover.
6. Describe five IRS-imposed tax penalties that could be levied against IRA participants.

Footnote

[1] The term *qualified plan* specifically and technically refers to employee plans meeting the requirements of Section 401 of the Internal Revenue Code, and does not relate to IRAs which are established under code Sections 219 and 408. If a plan is recognized officially by the IRS as meeting the requirements of these sections, it properly may be described as an "approved" plan.

Eligibility, Contributions and Deductibility

Chapter Two

Chapter Two
Objectives

After studying this chapter, you should be able to:

- Describe the eligibility requirements and contribution limits for the five types of IRA contributions;
- Outline what an allowable contribution is;
- Give three examples of how an excess contribution might occur, the consequences and how to cure it;
- Explain the difference between fully deductible, fully nondeductible and partially deductible IRA contributions;
- Explain a financial institution's responsibility in monitoring contributions; and
- Describe the types of available retirement savings plans.

Each of the five types of IRA contributions (contributory, spousal, third-party sponsored, SEP and rollover) has eligibility requirements defined by IRA law. In addition, IRA contributions are regulated by law in two ways: the amount that may be contributed and taken as a deduction, and the timing of the contributions.

Participants of contributory and third-party sponsored IRAs must meet age and compensation requirements. Participants in spousal IRAs must meet these and other requirements. Rollover contributions to IRAs may be made with the funds from either a lump-sum or a partial distribution from a qualified pension plan or other IRA. SEP eligibility requirements are set by employers within those specified by law. Other IRA restrictions include specified limits on contributions and deductibility for each type of IRA contribution, except rollovers. All IRA contributions are subject to timing restrictions.

If contribution limits are exceeded or timing restrictions not followed, an excess contribution may occur, which may incur one or more tax penalties. A participant can avoid one tax penalty by withdrawing the excess before filing the federal income tax return. Excess contributions may be cured by withdrawing the excess portion and interest, or by taking the tax penalty and undercontributing by the amount of the excess for the following taxable year.

While eligibility for IRA contributions is not changing, the deductibility of IRA contributions will be more complicated because it now depends on whether an individual is an active participant in a qualified pension plan. If an individual is an active participant in a qualified plan, then his or her tax filing status and adjusted gross income must be considered. If an individual is not an active participant, then his or her only eligibility requirements concern age and compensation.

In cases where a participant is covered by a qualified plan and earns more than a certain income, specific dollar limitations are set upon deductibility. Earnings on nondeductible contributions continue to receive tax-sheltered status.

The three tax-deferred retirement savings plans created by ERISA are IRAs, retirement annuities and retirement bonds. This chapter explains each type, and briefly describes the allowable investments available for each plan from the many different IRA sponsors.

Types of IRA Contributions

The following five basic types of IRA contributions may be made by participants:

- **Contributory**

  A type of IRA contribution made by individuals who set aside all or a portion of their yearly compensation. Also termed a regular or individual IRA contribution.

- **Spousal**

  A type of regular IRA contribution which enables a working spouse to establish an IRA for his or her spouse. Spousal IRA contributions were created by the Tax Reform Act of 1976.

- **Third-Party Sponsored**

  A type of IRA contribution made by an employer, a union or an employee association; also known as a Section 408(c) IRA. Contributions are made into the IRA accounts by the employer or association on behalf of the employees. Sponsors are free to be selective in their offerings; they may make IRA contributions for only certain categories of employees (for example, management personnel) if they wish.

- **SEP (Simplified Employee Pension Plan)**
A type of IRA plan created by the Revenue Act of 1978, also called a Section 408(k) IRA, in which an employer may provide retirement benefits by making contributions to employees' IRAs. SEPs are subject to certain nondiscrimination and eligibility requirements.

- **Rollover**
A type of IRA contribution that allows employees who receive a distribution from an employer's qualified plan or IRA to reinvest all or any portion of the funds in an IRA. Several types of rollovers are permitted.

Each type of IRA contribution is subject to restrictions concerning eligibility and contributions.

Eligibility

Most types of IRA contributions must satisfy two general requirements: participants must not exceed the maximum age during the tax year for which they are making contributions, and participants must have received compensation. Specific age and compensation requirements are shown in Chapter 1, Figure 1-4.

Age

There is no *minimum* age requirement for eligibility. However, for most types of IRA contributions, there is a *maximum* age restriction. A participant may not establish or contribute to a contributory or third-party sponsored IRA for or after the tax year in which the participant turns 70½. This limitation applies even if the participant is still receiving compensation at 70½ and insures that the IRA is used as a retirement savings program rather than as a tax-sheltered, estate-building device.

For example, if Harold Scott will be 70 in May, he may not contribute to an IRA for that taxable year (because he will turn 70½ in November of that same year). However, if Harold's 70th birthday falls on or after July 1, Harold would be eligible to contribute for that taxable year, but not for the following year.

Recall from Chapter 1 that there are three exceptions to the age 70½ limitation:
- spousal IRA contributions—For example, suppose John and Mary, husband and wife, file a joint tax return. John is 72 years old and is still working. Mary is 68 years old and has been retired for several years. John cannot contribute into his own IRA but may contribute up to the regular contributory limits on Mary's behalf.
- SEP contributions—The Technical Corrections Act of 1979 specifically requires employers to make SEP contributions for all eligible employees, including those over age 70½.
- rollover contributions—Rollover contributions can be made at any age. The Internal Revenue Service has issued a number of private letter rulings in support of rollovers made after age 70½. Participants who make rollover or SEP contributions who are over age 70½ are subject to the distribution rules and must begin to take at least minimum withdrawals.

Compensation

Participants base IRA contributions on their compensation. Figure 2-1 illustrates what is included and excluded in the concept of "compensation."

Under the compensation requirement persons either employed by a company or self-employed are eligible to make IRA contributions. However, persons in a partnership who have a financial interest but not a working interest in the partnership, such as silent partners, are not eligible.

Since IRA law distinguishes between compensation and income, IRA participants also must make this distinction. For example, Joe Koltz earns $1,000 in salary and $5,000 from various investments in one taxable year. Joe's income for that year totals $6,000. However, only the $1,000 salary

FIGURE 2-1
Types of Income

Compensation	Income Not Defined As Compensation
■ salaries	■ investment earnings
■ wages	■ interest from deposit accounts
■ professional fees	■ rent on buildings or real estate
■ sales commissions	■ investments with a financial interest that do not include a working interest (silent partnership)
■ compensation based on a percentage of profits	
■ commissions on insurance premiums	■ Social Security income
■ tips	■ early retirement income
■ bonuses	■ deferred compensation
■ self-employment income	■ unemployment compensation
■ alimony	■ disability pay

qualifies as compensation. Joe's $5,000 in investment income cannot be used to figure his contribution limit.

Eligibility by Type of Contribution

Although the general age and compensation requirements apply for most types of IRA contributions, each type also has its own specific eligibility rules.

Contributory or Regular IRA Contributions

An individual must meet both age and compensation requirements to be eligible to participate in an IRA. First, the individual cannot make contributions to an IRA for or after the taxable year in which he or she reaches age 70½. Second, the individual must receive compensation during the taxable year. For divorced spouses, alimony received during the tax year is considered compensation for IRA purposes. If the individual is ineligible to participate in an IRA, either because of age or lack of compensation, no contributions may be made. In fact, tax penalties may be imposed on any contribution that is not allowable.

Spousal IRA Contributions

The eligibility rules for spousal IRA contributions are slightly modified to accommodate married couples. Three basic requirements for spousal IRAs must be met by a compensated individual and a designated noncompensated spouse: age, compensation and filing a joint income tax return. In addition, spousal IRAs have three unique age and compensation rules:

- Regarding age limitations, no contribution may be made on behalf of any person 70½ or older, even if that person is working. The situation is different if one spouse is under 70½. In this case a spousal IRA contribution may be made into the younger spouse's account until he or she reaches 70½. It does not matter which spouse actually earns compensation so long as one spouse is under 70½ and the spousal contribution is made on behalf of the younger person. For example, Myron Hendricks has been making spousal IRA contributions for himself and his nonworking spouse, Martha. Myron turns 70½ this year and becomes ineligible to make contributions on his own behalf. If Myron and Martha file a joint tax return, Myron can contribute up to the regular contributory limits on Martha's behalf.

- If the nonworking spouse reaches age 70½ but the working spouse does not, the working spouse can continue contributions to his or her own IRA until reaching age 70½. For example, Sam Johnson, who is 67 this year, has been making spousal contributions for himself and his wife Sadie, who is not employed. Sadie turns 70½ this year. Sam may no longer contribute for Sadie after she turns 70½; however, Sam is still eligible to make contributions to an IRA for himself.
- One spouse must receive compensation during the year and the other spouse must elect to be considered noncompensated for spousal IRA contribution purposes. At one time, in order to be eligible for a spousal IRA contribution one spouse had to have no compensation for the taxable year. The Tax Reform Act of 1986 eliminated this requirement. Today, any spouse may elect to be treated as having had no compensation for that year for spousal IRA contribution purposes.

Third-Party Sponsored IRA Contributions [Section 408(c) IRAs]

The eligibility requirements for third-party sponsored contributions (Section 408(c) IRAs) are the same as those for regular IRA contributions or, if the sponsor's plan permits contributions to the nonworking spouse's IRA, the same as for the spousal IRA contributions.

Simplified Employee Pension Plans (SEPs) [Section 408(k)IRAs]

Several aspects of eligibility set IRA contributions under a SEP apart from other types of IRA contributions. One element concerns equitable treatment for all employees. Under a SEP, contributions for a given calendar year must be made on behalf of every employee who has attained age 21 and performed service for the employer during at least three of the immediately preceding five calendar years. An employer is not required to include employees whose total yearly compensation is less than $300. These are the most stringent eligibility requirements permitted by law.

However, the employer may choose to set more generous SEP eligibility requirements in order to provide benefits to a wider range of employees than the law requires. This can be done by establishing a lower age or fewer years of service as conditions of eligibility provided that such standards are applied uniformly to all employees. The owner-employee as well as the employees must meet the eligibility requirements. Also, a SEP contribution must be made for any employee 70½ or over who otherwise meets eligibility requirements.

Rollover Contributions

The eligibility requirements for a rollover IRA contribution differ somewhat from the requirements for a regular IRA contribution. To be eligible for a rollover IRA contribution, an individual must

receive a distribution either from a qualified pension plan or from another retirement savings plan (such as another IRA or a Keogh). Amounts eligible for rollover include:
- all employer contributions;
- deductible or pretax employee contributions; and
- all earnings.[1]

The distribution may be either a lump-sum or partial distribution.

Individuals are required to redeposit the distributed funds into another tax-sheltered account (rollover transaction) within 60 days after receiving a distribution from a pension plan, a retirement program or another IRA. Failure to roll over the distributed funds during this 60-day period will disqualify the participant from redepositing the funds into an IRA and nullify the participant's ability to defer the amount distributed from taxes.

An individual may receive a distribution from a qualified plan and use all or any portion of the funds to make a rollover contribution into an IRA without any frequency limitations. There are frequency limitations, however, if the funds came from another IRA. Recall from Chapter 1 that a direct transfer of funds from one IRA trustee to another IRA trustee may occur as often as the participant desires. However, the law restricts the frequency or timing of allowable rollover contributions between one IRA and another. An IRA participant is allowed to make one rollover—from one IRA to another IRA—every 12 months. This 12-month period begins at the time a distribution is made to the participant for rollover purposes.

For contributions rolled over after March 20, 1986, individuals must designate in writing their election to roll over all or any portion of a lump-sum or partial distribution. Furthermore, the individual is prohibited from revoking a rollover.

Lump-sum distribution. Under certain circumstances, an individual might receive a lump-sum distribution from a qualified pension plan. A *lump-sum distribution* is the total amount of an employee's vested benefits accrued in the pension plan. A lump-sum distribution can be received from an employer's qualified pension plan under any one of the following circumstances:
- termination of the plan;
- attainment of age 59½ by the employee;
- separation from service (employee leaves the employer because of retirement or to take another job);
- a self-employed person becomes disabled;
- death of the employee, with a surviving spouse receiving the distribution; or
- distribution from a Section 403(b) tax-sheltered annuity (custodial account).

In addition, an owner-employer may terminate his or her Keogh plan, take a premature distribution and roll it over into an IRA. In doing so, the owner-employer avoids taxes and penalties.

A participant who has received a lump-sum distribution under any of the preceding circumstances may take all or any portion of the funds from the lump-sum distribution and make a rollover contribution to an IRA. Also, if the qualified plan funds are kept in a separate conduit IRA, they may be rolled back into another qualified plan. The individual is free to make a rollover contribution to an IRA even if he or she is ineligible to participate in a contributory IRA. For example, Bob, a 72-year-old who is no longer working, receives a lump-sum distribution from his former employer. Bob can make a rollover contribution even though he is over 70½ and has no compensation. Furthermore, if Bob had received the distribution three years ago while still working, he could have made a rollover contribution to an IRA within 60 days of receipt in addition to being able to make a regular IRA contribution.

Partial distribution. In the past, to qualify for a rollover transaction, a participant had to receive all of the funds from the lump-sum distribution or plan termination within one taxable year. However, because of recent changes in IRA law, a partial distribution rollover from a qualified plan is now allowed. A *partial distribution* will qualify for rollover treatment when:
- the distribution is equal to 50% or more of the participant's credit in the plan; and
- the distribution is made for one of the following reasons:
  —death of the participant;
  —disability of the participant; or
  —separation from service (participant retires or leaves employer to take another job).

Rollovers from a contributory IRA to another IRA. All or part of an IRA containing only regular contributions may be rolled over into another IRA to which regular contributions are made. This means that contributions may continue to be made to the original IRA. This differs from a rollover from a qualified plan because the IRA created by a rollover from a qualified plan should not accept any further regular contributions. A rollover from a contributory IRA to another IRA may not be made more than once every 12 months from the date of the last rollover. This rule applies per IRA plan. For example, if several certificates of deposit are in the same IRA plan, each CD is not considered a separate IRA. In this case, a direct transfer could be used to move funds from such an IRA to another IRA as CDs mature. Recall that direct transfers have no frequency limitations.

Contributions

IRA law regulates contributions to IRAs in two ways: the amount that may be contributed (and taken as a deduction) and the timing of the contributions.

General Rules and Concerns

In addition to the previously discussed eligibility requirements of age and compensation, the allowable maximum amounts of contributions, timing of IRA deposits and the nature of those deposits define what are known as *allowable contributions*. This section covers the amount and timing rules of IRA deposits. Federal deposit insurance concerns about IRA deposits also are discussed. The nature and types of investments permitted and barred from retirement savings plans are detailed in the last section of this chapter.

Allowable Maximums

Limitations on the maximum allowable IRA contributions are defined as the lesser of either a stated dollar amount or a percentage of a participant's compensations (see Figure 2-2). The law does not mandate any minimum contribution amount.

Timing Requirements

IRA contributions must be made within a specified time period to apply to a particular year. The taxable year is the basis for determining the timing of a contribution. The *taxable year* for individuals is that period of time used as the basis for calculating

FIGURE 2-2
Allowable Contribution Limits

Contributory	$2,000 or 100% of compensation, whichever is less
Spousal	$2,250 or 100% of compensation, whichever is less (No more than $2,000 contributed to the account of either spouse.)
Third-Party Sponsored	Follows contributory or spousal limits, whichever is applicable
Rollover	No dollar limitations
SEPs	For 1987, $30,000 or 15% of compensation, whichever is less. Beginning 1988, this is subject to cost-of-living changes. An employee may contribute an additional $2,000 annually.

Note: Investment income *may not* be used in calculating compensation to figure contribution limitations.

their federal income tax returns. For most taxpayers, their taxable year is the same as a calendar year. Rollovers are the only type of contribution subject to different timing restrictions.

IRAs may be opened *after* the end of the taxable year if contributions are made during the *leeway period*, the time between the end of the calendar year and the date for filing of income tax returns (January 1 and April 15). Contributions made between January 1 and April 15 for the preceding year are considered to have been made as of December 31 of that preceding year. This leeway period is significant for IRA participants because it allows for greater flexibility in establishing and contributing to IRAs.

The last applicable day for an IRA for the preceding year is April 15. No further extension is allowed for opening or contributing to an IRA, even if the individual is granted an extension for filing his or her income tax. Thus, the leeway period automatically extends allowable contributions to the due date of the tax return. Even if an IRA participant files a return earlier than April 15, this leeway provision still remains in effect. The taxpayer can make a retroactive IRA contribution between the earlier filing date and April 15 and take advantage of the tax benefits by filing an amended return.

To illustrate the use of the leeway period, consider the case of John Jenkins. John earned $19,000 in 19X1, the first year he had an IRA, and he expects to earn the same amount in 19X2, the second year. By December 31 of 19X1, John has not contributed any amount to his IRA for that taxable year. On February 2 of 19X2, John contributes $2,000 to his IRA for 19X1, the first taxable year. On May 4, he contributes $1,000 to be applied to his second year IRA contributions. Although John contributes $3,000 during 19X2—far in excess of the $2,000 allowable maximum for his IRA—John's contributions are nevertheless allowable because he took advantage of the leeway period for his first year's contribution.

As another example, Bertha Morse establishes her contributory IRA account on January 22 of 19X2 and contributes $1,000 of her part-time salary to it for 19X1, the previous taxable year. In May, Bertha turns age 70½ and is no longer eligible to contribute to an IRA. This development does not adversely affect Bertha's contribution since the law enables her to establish her IRA and make contributions to it during the leeway period in one year for the previous year, and Bertha was not age 70½ until 19X2, the latter taxable year.

Except for rollovers from a contributory IRA to another IRA, participants are free to establish and contribute to any number of IRAs as frequently as desired, provided they follow rules regarding eligibility and contribution limits per taxable year. Contributions do not need to be in the form of one single deposit. Contributions may be made as often as the participant desires, provided that contributions for a taxable year are completed by the following April 15.

IRA law also permits certain eligible participants to skip contributions for a number of years. For contributory, spousal and third-party sponsored IRAs, each year's contribution is voluntary. An IRA deposit for one year does not require these participants to make deposits in subsequent years. However, an individual *must* cease contributions if he or she becomes ineligible, such as through unemployment. The IRA may be resumed in any year in which the participant again becomes eligible to make contributions.

Federal Deposit Insurance Concerns
Insurance protection is a special concern for IRA owners. Because IRA funds may grow to very large figures over several decades, and because insurance of accounts coverage is limited, participants may need multiple IRA accounts at different financial institutions to receive full insurance of accounts coverage.

Similarly, an individual who receives a lump-sum distribution of substantial size may wish to divide the distribution and roll it over into IRAs in different institutions to assure full insurance of accounts coverage.

The Federal Deposit Insurance Corporation

(FDIC), the Federal Savings and Loan Insurance Corporation (FSLIC) and the National Credit Union Administration (NCUA) were created by Congress to insure the accounts of its members. Insurance-of-accounts coverage by the FSLIC, FDIC or NCUA on IRAs and qualified plans is separate from that on any other accounts the participant may have at the same institution. Furthermore, if the participant has both an IRA and a qualified plan account at the same institution, each is separately insured up to $100,000.

Allowable Contributions by Type

Some types of IRAs allow larger annual contributions than others. In this section, the contribution rules that apply to each of the five types of IRAs are covered.

Regular Contributions

IRA law limits allowable contributions per taxable year for contributory IRAs to the lesser of $2,000 or 100% of compensation. Individuals who earn more than $2,000 per year may contribute to a maximum limit of $2,000. Individuals who earn less than $2,000 per year are restricted to a maximum of 100% of their compensation.

In the case of married couples, if both spouses are employed and eligible, each may establish a separate IRA. The limitation on allowable contributions applies separately to each participant's account. Income tax deductions for each spouse are determined separately; these are totalled if the couple files a joint tax return. For example, if each spouse had compensation over $2,000, the total allowable contributions (and deductions provided neither is an active participant) would be $4,000 ($2,000 per each spouse's IRA). The separate regular contributions made to the respective IRAs of two working spouses are not to be confused with spousal IRA contributions.

Spousal Contributions
Total allowable spousal contributions are limited. The current amount is $2,250 or 100% of the working spouse's compensation, whichever is less. IRA contributions may be divided between the spouses' accounts in any way the participants choose. However, not more than $2,000 can be contributed to the account of either spouse. Contributions to any spousal account exceeding the $2,000 are considered excess contributions and are subject to a tax penalty.

For example, Gene and Betty Tyrol have established IRAs with the intent to fund them by spousal contributions. During a single taxable year, Betty earned $15,000 in compensation and Gene had no compensation. In order to gain full advantage of their spousal IRA's tax benefits, Betty could contribute up to $2,000 to her account and up to $250 to Gene's account, or vice versa. As long as not more than $2,000 is contributed on either Betty or Gene's behalf, the $2,250 may be divided between their accounts in any way they choose.

When both spouses work, but one earns only a small amount, the couple can choose between opening two regular IRAs or a spousal IRA depending upon which alternative is more favorable. For example, assume Carol Jones earned $100 from a part-time job in 1986, and Mark Jones had compensation of $20,000. Mark can make a $2,000 deductible IRA contribution for himself, and Carol may make a $100 deductible IRA contribution for herself, for a total IRA deduction on their joint return of $2,100. Alternatively, Carol and Mark may elect to treat Carol, for the purpose of making a spousal IRA contribution, as having no compensation. This alternative increases their *total* IRA contribution and deduction to $2,250. The election to treat a spouse as having no compensation is made by specifying, on a joint return, that a spousal IRA contribution has been made.

Compensation status may change from year to year. This means that the status of contributions also may change: a couple may choose to use a spousal IRA in some years, and a contributory IRA in other years.

Financial institutions must structure spousal IRAs as two separate accounts. This is necessary because the law does not allow jointly owned IRA accounts.

Third-Party Sponsored Contributions
The same contribution limitation rules ($2,000 or 100% of compensation, whichever is less) that apply to contributory IRA contributions also pertain to third-party sponsored contributions. If the sponsor's plan also permits contributions to the nonworking spouse's IRA, the limitation rules for spousal IRA contributions (the lesser of $2,250 or 100% of compensation, and no more than $2,000 to the account of either spouse) are applicable.

If the employer's contribution is less than $2,000, then the employee may contribute the difference to a regular IRA account. For example, if Bud Seikirk receives contributions of $1,000 to a Section 408(c) IRA from his union, Bud may contribute another $1,000 to his own IRA. However, if Bud's union were to contribute $2,000 for him in a taxable year, he could not contribute any more into his own IRA for that taxable year.

Amounts contributed on behalf of an employee are taxed as compensation. The contribution amount is included in an employee's taxable income. Also, such contributions are subject to Social Security and unemployment taxes. Employees treat third-party sponsored contributions on their federal income tax returns in the same way as if they had made the contributions themselves.

SEPs
A higher level of contributions is allowed for SEPs than for other types of IRAs. The yearly contribution limit to a SEP agreement IRA is $32,000 ($30,000 from the employer and $2,000 from the employee). The limit for employees over 70½ is $30,000, all of which must come from the employer because employees over 70½ may not make an additional $2,000 contribution to their own IRA. In addition, the employer can base the contribution only on the first $200,000 of a participant's salary.[2] Thus an employer may make payments to each eligible employee's IRA of up to 15% of an employee's compensation (maximum $200,000) or $30,000 ($200,000 X 15%), whichever is less.

Under a SEP the employer's contribution percentage must be the same for all employees because IRA law imposes nondiscrimination requirements. These include provisions for a written allocation formula which determines employer contributions to the employee's IRA each year. The contribution formula must be applied uniformly to all employees who are covered by the plan. In the case of employees over 70½, the employer is required to continue making contributions as long as the person is otherwise eligible. Also, the contribution percentage must not discriminate in favor of any employee who is an officer, shareholder or self-employed individual, or is highly compensated.

The SEP eligibility and contribution rules that apply to employers are separate from the regular and spousal IRA contributions that participants may be eligible for. Also, participants may make regular IRA contributions into the same IRAs into which their employers are making the SEP contributions. This explains why an annual SEP contribution of $32,000 is permitted when the employer can contribute only $30,000. However, employees who are over 70½ may not make the additional $2,000 contribution since they would not be permitted to do so under regular IRA rules.

Since a SEP is an IRA, employer contributions to a SEP become immediately and fully vested for the employee and regular IRA rules apply. In addition, an employer may not prohibit an employee from withdrawing funds from the plan or make retention of the funds in the plan a condition of employment. However, all IRA distribution rules apply and should an employee withdraw funds from the plan before reaching the age of 59½ or becoming disabled, he or she would be subject to the IRS premature distribution penalty.

Elective-deferral arrangements. The Tax Reform Act of 1986 made an important tax change relating to SEP agreements affecting small firms (25 employees or less). The Act allows for employees of such small firms to shelter some of their income from taxation by making voluntary contributions under the employer's SEP.

Technically, these arrangements are called *elective-*

deferral arrangements. Employees can defer up to $7,000 of annual salary to the plan in addition to the employer's contributions. The deferrals are considered additional employer contributions because the amounts are counted into the 15% or $30,000 limitations on SEP contributions. Contributions remain tax-sheltered until withdrawn.

In order for such an elective-deferral arrangement to take effect, at least half of the employees in the plan must agree to elect the deferrals. Elective-deferral arrangements are explained in more detail in Chapter 5.

Making both SEP and Keogh contributions. An employee also may have income from self-employment. In this case, the person may have both a SEP and a Keogh. (A Keogh is a retirement plan for self-employed persons.) However, the IRS Model SEP agreement that many institutions use to establish a SEP does not allow for this. A different SEP agreement that allows both a Keogh and SEP would be required. Contributions to both the Keogh and the SEP could not, in the aggregate, exceed contribution limits of 25% of compensation, or $30,000, whichever is less. This situation also is explained more fully in Chapter 5.

Rollovers
Unlike all other types of IRA contributions, the law does not set any dollar or percentage limitations on the amount of a rollover contribution. However, rollover contributions have several significant aspects regarding where the funds came from, in what form they were received and how they might be handled.

Sources and placement of rollover funds. An employee may roll over funds to an IRA from a qualified pension plan, a Keogh plan, a retirement annuity or another IRA. Rollovers from a qualified plan may not include after-tax employee contributions, but may include employer contributions and the earnings from both employer and employee contributions. An employee may choose to roll over all or any portion of the eligible funds into an IRA. Note that a rollover distribution is called a rollover contribution when the funds are redeposited into another tax-sheltered account.

Rollover funds and contributory IRA funds generally are not combined into one account. Although IRA law neither sanctions nor prohibits the combining of IRAs in this manner, as a practical matter, few trustees permit such a combination. The IRA law specifies that a conduit IRA will not remain a conduit if regular contributions are made to it. This means that once a distribution from a qualified plan is mixed with regular IRA contributions, it no longer can be redeposited into another qualified plan. Thus, most IRA trustees prohibit combinations so that participants are protected from mistakenly forfeiting the conduit advantages of such rollover contributions.

Noncash distributions. The Revenue Act of 1978 gives recipients of noncash distributions the power to convert the property into cash before rolling over all or any portion of the distribution into an IRA. Formerly, the conversion of such noncash property had to be accomplished either before it left the distributing plan or after it was delivered to the rollover IRA trustee. Since the taxable year 1979, the recipient of noncash property has been able to make a bona fide sale and roll over the proceeds into an IRA. If all the proceeds from the sale are rolled over, no taxable gain or loss is realized in the eyes of the law. However, if only a partial rollover of the sale proceeds occurs, the participant must report the portion retained as ordinary income.

Mix of noncash and cash properties. If a distribution consists of both cash and noncash property, the recipient can choose to allocate any amount of cash and noncash property to the rollover. This decision must be made no later than the filing date of the income tax return and once made is irrevocable. If no such decision is made within the allotted time, the rollover is prorated between the amount of the cash distribution received and the fair market value of the noncash property received, valued as of the date of distribution. Recipients of noncash property are not permitted to effect a rollover by substituting cash for the property's value; the property cannot be retained and must be properly sold to qualify for a valid rollover into an IRA.

Excess Contributions

IRA law prohibits excess contributions, and the IRS may impose a tax penalty on participants who make excess contributions. There are four situations in which IRA contributions would be called excess. First, an individual might contribute more than the allowable amount for a tax year. This could occur for two reasons: either the dollar limitations or the percentage of income restrictions were exceeded. Examples include contributing over $2,000 to a regular IRA or contributing over 100% of compensation. Here, any amount above the maximum would be classified as an excess contribution.

Second, an individual might contribute funds that are not based on compensation. For instance, if someone did not receive any income that the IRS considers compensation (see Figure 2-1), he or she would not be able to contribute into an IRA. For example, someone who had no compensation would not be able to use funds received as a birthday gift to make an IRA contribution. In fact, any amount this person contributes to an IRA would be treated as an excess contribution. Note, however, that although the contribution must be *based* on compensation, the participant's actual contribution can come from any source, including borrowed funds.

Third, an individual might not meet the personal criteria for people who may contribute; for example, a person over the age of 70½ is not eligible. Here, the entire amount from an ineligible person would be called an excess contribution.

Fourth, all or part of the funds from a rollover might be ineligible. An excess rollover contribution would occur if the participant did not reinvest his or her distribution in a rollover within 60 days. In this case the distribution would no longer qualify for rollover treatment. Also, if the participant tried to roll over portions of a distribution from a pension plan representing the employee's own after-tax contributions to that plan, an excess rollover contribution would occur. In this case, the after-tax dollars cannot be rolled over.

The IRS considers the individual IRA owner to be responsible for any excess contribution penalty taxes. Thus, no liability is incurred by the financial institution that accepted the funds nor by any other IRA trustee.

There are several ways for participants to avoid

penalties or to correct actions that might lead the IRS to claim that an excess contribution has been made. These methods also are known as *curing* excess contributions and are explained more fully later in this section.

Tax penalty

An excess contribution is subject to a nondeductible 6% tax penalty. The excess amount of the contribution must be included as taxable income for the taxable year in which it was contributed, and federal income tax is due on any of the earnings received from the excess. For purposes of calculating the penalty, the amount of the excess is determined as of the end of the taxable year. In no case can the penalty exceed 6% of the value of the account at that time. The penalty is imposed for each taxable year that the excess remains uncured.

Depending on the timing, amount and how the excess contribution is cured, the earnings on the excess contribution may or may not be allowed to remain in the IRA account. If the earnings on the excess contribution must be removed to correct the excess, then the participant will pay a 10% premature distribution penalty on the interest if he or she is under age 59½ and is not disabled. Also, for contributions over $2,250 that must be removed after the participant's federal income tax due date, both the 6% excess contribution penalty and the 10% premature distribution penalty would apply.

Curing Excess Contributions for Most Types of IRAs

For most types of IRAs, an IRA participant who has contributed an excess amount can cure the excess in the following ways:
- removing the excess, including earnings on the excess;

- not withdrawing anything and applying the excess to next year's contribution; or
- removing the excess but not removing the earnings on the excess.

When the tax penalties apply and how to cure excess contributions are dependent on the following factors:
- whether the excess is cured before or after the participant's due date for filing his or her federal income tax return;
- if the participant can redesignate the excess as a contribution for a later year; and
- if the contribution exceeded $2,250.

Curing excess rollover contributions and curing employer-made SEP contributions have exceptions. These exceptions are explained later.

Before the participant's tax return due date (including extensions). A participant can cure any excess contribution before the due date for filing his or her federal income tax return by:
- withdrawing the excess, including earnings on the excess; and
- reporting the earnings on the excess as income for the year the excess was made and paying a 10% premature distribution penalty on the earnings from the excess only.

The participant will not be charged the 6% excess contribution tax. Therefore, curing the excess before the tax return due date is the participant's least costly remedy.

After the participant's tax return due date. If the participant's due date has passed, the participant will need to determine if he or she is eligible for an IRA contribution for a subsequent tax year. If eligible and the maximum contribution for the next

year has not been made yet, then the participant would:
- redesignate the excess as a contribution for a later year by amending the prior year's tax return; and
- leave the earnings on the excess in the IRA and pay a 6% penalty for the excess contribution for each year it remains as an excess in the IRA.

Excess contributions may be applied only to subsequent years. An excess contribution cannot be cured by applying it against prior allowable contributions that fell below the maximum IRA limitations for participants' contributions. If the participant is not eligible for a subsequent year's IRA contribution, and the total contributions for the year did not exceed $2,250, then the participant can cure the excess by:
- withdrawing the excess amount; and
- leaving the earnings on the excess in the IRA and paying a 6% penalty for each year it remained as an excess in the IRA.

If the participant is not eligible for a subsequent year's IRA contribution, and the total contributions for the year exceeded $2,250, then the participant can cure the excess by:
- withdrawing the excess amount and paying a 10% premature distribution penalty on the excess if he or she is under age 59½ and not disabled; and
- leaving the earnings on the excess in the IRA and paying a 6% penalty for each year it remained as an excess in the IRA.

Therefore, curing an excess contribution over $2,250 after the tax return date will cost the participant the most. Financial institution employees might tell their IRA customers not to put more than $2,250 in total contributions into their IRAs for any one tax year. If this happens, customers will want to remove the excess contribution before their tax return due date to cure it in the least costly way.

Curing Excess Contributions for SEPs and Rollovers
Excess SEP or rollover contributions can be cured in ways similar to the other types of IRA contributions. However, there are some exceptions to the tax penalties and curing methods.

Curing excess SEP contributions. If an employer contributes more to an employee's SEP than the employer is allowed to deduct, the employee must cure the excess in the manner previously described with one exception. If the employee's tax return due date has passed, the 10% premature distribution penalty will not apply if the withdrawal does not exceed the lesser of either the employer contribution or $30,000. Beginning in 1988, this amount will be adjusted for inflation.

Proposed regulations would provide an alternate way to correct an excess SEP contribution that was caused by an employer's error, by allowing the excess to be credited to another IRA of the employee.

Curing excess rollover contributions. If an excess rollover contribution occurs, the participant corrects it in the same manner as he or she would for regular IRAs, with one exception. If the excess rollover occurred because incorrect information was given to the participant from the source of the rollover, then the excess can be withdrawn without liability for income tax or the 10% premature distribution penalty.

Deductibility of Contributions

The Tax Reform Act of 1986 did not alter the *eligibility* requirements for IRA participation. However, the *deductibility* of those contributions may be limited, depending on a number of factors pertaining to the participant:
- status as an active participant in a qualified pension plan;
- tax filing status (single, married filing jointly, married filing separately); and
- adjusted gross income.

Depending on these three factors, individuals' IRA contributions will be one of three kinds: fully deductible, fully nondeductible or partially deductible.

Persons not considered active participants in a qualified pension plan may continue to make fully deductible IRA contributions. However, individuals defined as active participants will find the deductibility of their contributions subject to limitations dependent on their adjusted gross incomes (see Figure 2-3).

Recall from Chapter 1 that a qualified pension plan includes any of the following IRS-approved plans:
- a qualified pension or defined-benefit plan, profit sharing or money purchase plan, or stock bonus plan (an employer contributes retirement benefits for employees to an IRS-approved plan and receives a tax deduction for contributions);
- a qualified annuity, including Keoghs (retirement plans approved for self-employed persons)

FIGURE 2-3
IRA Contributions for Active Participants

If your filing status is:	and you are in an employer-sponsored qualified plan with an adjusted gross income of:		
Single	$25,000 or less	$25,001 to $34,999	$35,000 or more
Married, filing jointly	$40,000 or less	$40,001 to $49,999	$50,000 or more
Married, filing singly	$0	Under $10,000	$10,000 or more
Your IRA contribution is:	Fully Deductible	Partially Deductible	Not Deductible

and 401(k) plans (salary reduction plans, based on voluntary payroll deductions of pretax dollars of a specific percentage of an employee's salary to one or more employer-selected investment plans);
- a government retirement plan;
- an annuity contract purchased by a tax-exempt organization;
- a union plan; or
- a SEP.

The IRS defines an *active participant* as an individual included in any of the following situations:
- In a defined-benefit plan, a person who was included under the eligibility provisions of the plan for any portion of the plan year ending with or within such individual's taxable year.
- In a profit-sharing or stock bonus plan, if a forfeiture was allocated to his or her account as of a date in the taxable year or if a contribution was added to his or her account in such taxable year.
- In a money purchase plan, if, under the terms of the plan, employer contributions or forfeitures

should have been allocated to the individual's account within the plan year ending with or within the individual's taxable year.
- If an employee actively participated in a pension plan in one job but was also employed in a second job that did not offer a pension plan, then the employee could not establish an IRA based only on the second job.
- If an employee made voluntary or mandatory contributions to a qualified pension plan, he or she was an active participant for the taxable year when the contributions were made.

The employer indicates whether the employee is an active participant on Form W-2. Employees receive their Form W-2 early each year from their employers. The form is used to report to the employee and the IRS wages earned and taxes withheld for the previous year.

Fully Deductible IRA Contributions

Two categories of individuals continue to qualify for fully deductible contributions, up to the allowable dollar limits for the particular type of IRA: individuals not covered under a qualified pension plan and individuals covered under a qualified plan but with an adjusted gross income below a certain dollar amount. *Adjusted gross income* (AGI) includes not only compensation, but also interest and investment income, and Social Security benefits *minus* certain adjustments (such as moving expenses, contributions to Keoghs, early withdrawal penalties and alimony). IRA contributions are *not* subtracted in calculating AGI.

Fully deductible IRA contributions may be made by individuals who are considered active participants and who are:

- single, with an AGI of $25,000 or less;
- married, filing jointly, with a combined AGI of $40,000 or less; or
- married, filing separately, with an AGI of $0.

Fully Nondeductible IRA Contributions

Nondeductible IRA contributions may not be deducted from an individual's tax return; however, such contributions are valid in all other respects. Nondeductible contributions are keyed to income level limits and designed to prevent higher income taxpayers from sheltering their income with an IRA deduction.

Individuals who are covered by a qualified pension plan and earn an AGI above certain income level limits may make only nondeductible IRA contributions. Those individuals fall into the following categories:
- single, covered by a qualified plan, with an AGI over $35,000;
- married, filing jointly, with one or both of the spouses covered by a qualified plan and with the couple reporting a combined AGI over $50,000 (neither regular nor spousal IRA is deductible); or
- married, filing separately, the covered individual with an AGI over $10,000. (The spouse who is not an active participant and who files separately may make a fully deductible contribution.)

Nondeductible contributions must be designated as such on an individual's tax return. Individuals will be required to report amounts of IRA contributions, whether the contributions were deductible or nondeductible, any IRA withdrawal amounts and the total IRA balance at the end of a taxable year.

The designation of a contribution as nondeductible may be made or changed at any time up to the filing date for federal income tax returns (April 15). Also, any nondeductible amounts may be withdrawn before that date without IRS penalty if the individual wishes not to make any nondeductible contributions to an IRA account. Contributions also may be designated as nondeductible, even if deductibility is allowed by law, if the individual wishes to do so.

Failure to designate a nondeductible contribution as such may cause the contribution to be taxed *again* upon withdrawal: the IRS may choose to treat any undesignated contribution as a deductible one, and thus subject the amount to taxation.

Earnings on any nondeductible contributions remain tax-sheltered until withdrawn. If an IRA includes both deductible and nondeductible contributions, then any withdrawals will be treated as partly deductible and partly nondeductible funds. Upon withdrawal, the nondeductible portion will not be taxed; the deductible portion will be taxed.

Although changes may be made to IRA contributions and status before April 15 without incurring tax penalties from the IRS, the individual may still need to pay any early withdrawal penalties to the institution, and must report any earnings or gains attributable to the IRA contribution as income for the taxable year in which the contribution is made.

Partially Deductible IRA Contributions (Phase-Out Deductions)

Specific deductibility limits will apply when individuals are active participants in a qualified plan and fall within particular income limits. Explanations of who is eligible for a partially deductible contribution, and how the deduction is figured, are covered below. When calculating the deductible IRA portion, answers not a multiple of $10 should be rounded up to the next highest $10, and nondeductible amounts not a multiple of $10 should be rounded down to the next lowest $10.

- Single individuals, covered by a qualified plan, with AGI between $25,000 and $35,000, reduce the $2,000 regular IRA limit by $20 for every $100 of AGI between $25,000 and $35,000.
- Married individuals filing jointly, with one or both of the spouses covered by a qualified plan, and with a combined AGI between $40,000 and $50,000, reduce the $2,000 regular IRA limit for each eligible spouse by $20 for every $100 of AGI between $40,000 and $50,000. To figure spousal IRA deductibility, reduce the $2,250 spousal IRA limit by $22.50 for every $100 of AGI between $40,000 and $50,000.
- Married individuals filing separately who are active participants will phase out deductions with an AGI between $0 and $10,000. To figure deductibility, these people reduce the regular $2,000 IRA limit by $20 for each $100 between $0 and $10,000.

For example, Ruth Reschke is single, and is covered under her company's profit sharing plan. Ruth has an AGI of $27,000 for the taxable year. To figure Ruth's deductibility, the $2,000 regular IRA limit must be reduced $20 for every $100 between $25,000 and $27,000. This equals $400. Therefore, Ruth's deductible IRA contribution would be $2,000 *minus* $400, or $1,600. Ruth may contribute up to $1,600 and report it as fully deductible, or she may make a contribution of up to $2,000, reporting $1,600 as her deductible contribution, and the remaining $400 as her nondeductible contribution.

Participants may choose, if they wish, to contribute *only* the deductible portion of their IRA, in order to keep the status of their IRA as fully deductible both now and upon retirement.

Limits on deductibility apply equally to two compensated spouses. For example, if a couple has a combined AGI of $44,000, then the deduction limit *for each spouse* is $1,200. Each spouse may deduct only up to $1,200, even if the other spouse takes a smaller or even no deduction.

Trustees' Liability

As IRA trustees, financial institutions are responsible for monitoring IRAs to insure the contributions made during a single taxable year do not exceed the dollar limitations within that specific sponsor's accounts. The monitoring requirements for dollar limitations are an extremely important aspect of an institution's IRA operations. Monitoring requirements for dollar limitations do not require the trustee to relate the limitations to the actual amount of compensation. Participants themselves are responsible for contributing no more than allowed under the percentage of compensation limits. Furthermore, trustees are not liable to indicate whether a contribution or any portion thereof is deductible or nondeductible; that responsibility lies with the participant.

Because of the leeway period given for making contributions, some financial institutions establish a means of relating participants' contributions made before April 15 of any year to the taxable year for which they are intended in order to monitor effectively the dollar limitations. For instance, the institution could require the customer to designate the year for which the contribution is being made. When the deposit is taken, an IRA participant may appear to be making an excess contribution when, in fact, he or she is taking advantage of the leeway provisions.

Retirement Savings Plans

When making plans for retirement, an individual must first consider his or her possible sources of retirement income. These could include Social Security, savings and other investments, pension plans, Keoghs and the various retirement savings plans. The individual should assess whether these sources of income will provide sufficient income to meet retirement needs.

The three tax-deferred retirement savings plans created by ERISA are IRAs, retirement annuities and retirement bonds. Each savings plan has its advantages and disadvantages. Each individual should weigh the options in light of his or her own retirement needs. Any individual planning for retirement should figure the total or periodic amounts of income that will be needed during retirement, and whether that amount will be available from current sources of income. Other factors to consider carefully when deciding which retirement savings plan will best provide needed income include the following:

- whether funds will be available if an emergency arises;
- whether a guaranteed return on investments is necessary; and

- whether a higher rate of return is worth a greater risk.

Numerous investment possibilities are available to retirement savings plan participants. Allowable investments, as well as investments barred from retirement savings plans, are depicted in Figure 2-4. It is important to note that institutions without trust powers and which do not offer self-directed IRAs are limited to time and savings deposits at their institution.

IRA Sponsors

IRA contributions may be invested in a variety of options and be placed with a number of different sponsors:
- financial institutions (savings and loan institutions or banks);
- insurance companies;
- corporation offerings to stockholders;
- employers;
- credit unions;
- money market and other mutual funds; and
- stock brokerage houses.

Savings institution IRAs are often offered in the form of certificates of deposit. Certificates may have either a *fixed rate*, that is, a guaranteed rate of return until the certificate matures, or a *variable rate* with no limitations on how often the rate of return may change.

Institutions offer a wide variety of types of deposits, rates and services. One of the most widely chosen IRA options is the 18-month certificate (authorized as of December 1, 1981). Additional deposits may be accepted to such certificates. This flexibility feature allows a participant to spread out

FIGURE 2-4
Allowed and Barred Investments for IRAs

Allowed IRA Investments	Barred IRA Investments
Bonds	Collectibles:
Stocks	artworks
Money market instruments	rugs
Mutual funds	antiques
Insurance annuities	metals
Government securities	gems
Government agency notes	stamps
Treasury bills	alcoholic beverages
Certificates of deposit	Tangible personal property

Stocks:
  growth
  high-yield
  blue-chip
	Coins other than "American Eagle" or any fashioned into jewelry

Bonds:
  corporate
  convertible
  discount
  high-yield	

"American Eagle" gold and silver coins (U.S. Treasury-minted)	

contributions over the course of the year, rather than making a single lump-sum contribution. The participant may deposit as much or as little as he or she chooses, within the prescribed limits.

If an individual decides to invest in an IRA at a savings institution, the terms, rates of interest, permissible additions, minimum deposits and penalties of various plans should be compared. A participant also must be aware of the time periods covered by the certificates. The term of a certificate may limit the rollover of IRA funds into a different retirement plan.

Mutual fund companies and brokerage firms also offer IRAs with a variety of investment possibilities; however, fees are often charged for maintenance of such IRAs. In addition, fees may be charged for sales commissions, such as for the buying or selling of securities, or for transferring IRA money from one type of fund to another in order to take advantage of changing interest rates.

Federal associations also have limited authority to offer self-directed IRAs and Keoghs. Basically, associations are permitted to invest IRA funds *only* in the association's own accounts, deposits, obligations or securities, *or* to invest at the direction of the customer. Association employees *may not* exercise any investment discretion, or provide any investment advice concerning an IRA's assets.

Federal associations shall include the following language in bold type on the first page of any contract documents:

> Funds invested pursuant to this agreement are not insured by the Federal Savings and Loan Insurance Corporation (FSLIC) merely because the trustee or custodian is an institution the accounts of which are covered by such insurance. Only investments *in the accounts* of such an institution are insured by the FSLIC, subject to its rules and regulations.

This statement is intended to make customers who have self-directed IRAs at an FSLIC-insured association aware that any customer-directed investments outside of the association will not be insured.

Starting with 1987, IRA investments in "American Eagle" gold and silver coins are allowable. The U.S. Treasury began minting these coins in October 1986. Such coins are not allowable as IRA investments if they are in the form of jewelry. In addition, the IRA participant may not take possession of any such coins in an IRA: the coins must be held by a custodian, and any storage fees charged by the custodian must be paid for by the participant.

Retirement Annuities

Retirement annuities are offered only by life insurance companies. An *annuity* is usually a contract in which the participant makes regular annual payments (or *premiums*) for an established time period. Upon *maturity*, that is, the end of the stated time period, the insurer provides an annual payment of accumulated benefits to the participant, beginning upon retirement and continuing until death of the participant. An *endowment contract* is similar to an annuity. However an endowment provides for a guaranteed sum, or *face value*. The participant is insured for the face value of the agreement until maturity. The *principal sum*, or the value written into the policy, is paid upon maturity.

Premiums paid by retirement annuity participants are tax-deductible only to a limited extent. Only the amount of the premiums that becomes a part of the retirement savings program is tax-deductible. Insurance company fees and death benefits are *not* tax-deductible. Otherwise, retirement annuities offer the same tax benefits as IRAs.[3]

Retirement Bonds

Prior to May 1, 1982, an individual could purchase a *retirement bond*, issued by the U.S. Government. Although the U.S. Treasury has discontinued the sale of these bonds, they are still a part of many retirement plan portfolios. The retirement bonds continue to earn interest at a rate set by Congress. Rules pertaining to the distribution and redemption of such bonds continue to apply.[4]

Summary

In general, the eligibility requirements for most types of IRAs specify that to participate in an IRA, an individual must not contribute for the tax years during or after attaining age 70½ and must receive earned income or compensation. However, an individual may make rollover or SEP contributions after age 70½. Compensation includes salaries, wages, commissions, tips and bonuses but does not include earnings from interest or rental fees.

An individual becomes eligible for a rollover IRA upon receiving either a partial or a lump-sum distribution from a pension plan. A partial distribution is equal to 50% or more of a plan's assets, and the distribution is made because of disability, death or separation from service. A lump-sum distribution may occur because of plan termination, attainment of age 59½, separation from service, death or disability. All or any portion of either a partial or a lump-sum distribution may be rolled over to an IRA. IRA law has established maximum limits for contributions to a IRA and for the amount of income deduction that may be taken on a participant's federal income tax return. Except for rollovers, all types of IRAs are subject to contribution limits. Contributions must be made within the specified time restrictions, usually the taxable year plus the leeway period.

The Internal Revenue Service has mandated a 6%

tax penalty on excess IRA contributions. An IRA participant may use the leeway period to make adjustments to the yearly contribution amount. To cure excess contributions, the excess amount and interest on it may be withdrawn or the tax penalty may be taken and the participant may redesignate the excess amount to a subsequent year.

Individuals defined as active participants in qualified pension plans are not restricted from establishing or contributing to an IRA. However, for tax purposes, the deductibility of such contributions may be limited, depending on an individual's tax filing status and adjusted gross income.

A participant must determine whether he or she is an active participant, indicate whether all or any portion of an IRA contribution is deductible or nondeductible and be responsible for any excess contributions. Employers report employees' active participant status on the W-2 Form. Financial institutions are required to monitor each participant's total contributions in dollar amounts for the taxable year, but are not responsible for determining if an individual's contribution is deductible or nondeductible.

The three tax-deferred retirement savings plans created by ERISA are IRAs, retirement annuities and retirement bonds. A wide variety of IRA investments are allowable under current law and are available from a multitude of different kinds of sponsors in addition to financial institutions.

Chapter Questions

1. To what kinds of income does the term "compensation" refer under IRA law? Give at least three examples to support your answer.
2. What are the eligibility requirements for the following types of IRA contributions:
   a. contributory
   b. spousal
   c. third-party sponsored
   d. SEP
   e. rollover
3. For the following types of contributions, what are the permitted amounts that may be contributed? Be sure to include the dollar and percentage limitations.
   a. contributory
   b. spousal
   c. third-party sponsored
   d. SEP
4. What is an excess contribution? Give three examples of how an excess contribution may occur, the consequences and how it may be cured.
5. Which individuals are eligible to make fully deductible IRA contributions?
6. Which individuals may make only nondeductible contributions?
7. What are the dollar ranges for incomes that fall under the partially deductible category if the individuals are covered by a qualified pension plan?
   a. single
   b. married filing jointly
   c. married filing separately
8. How is the deductible portion of a contribution calculated?
9. Describe an IRA trustee's responsibility for monitoring contributions.

10. List several factors that individuals planning for their retirement should consider.
11. Who can offer retirement annuities? How are annuities and endowment contracts different?

Footnotes

[1] IRC Section 402(a)(5)(b)
[2] IRC Section 408(k)(3)(c)(i)
[3] For further information regarding the rules governing retirement annuities, see IRC Section 408(b).
[4] For further information regarding the rules governing retirement bonds, see IRC Section 409.

Distributions

**Chapter
Three**

Chapter Three Objectives

After studying this chapter, you should be able to:

- Describe the options a participant who is at least 59½ has for taking allowable distributions;
- Describe the situations in which allowable distributions may be taken before age 59½;
- Describe how nondeductible IRA contributions will affect IRA distributions;
- Identify the types of tax-deferred rollover contributions;
- Explain the difference between actual and constructive distributions; and
- Outline the tax consequences for premature distributions and underdistributions.

DISTRIBUTIONS ARE withdrawals from retirement plans. To insure that a participant uses IRA funds for retirement, IRA law has established certain timing restrictions on IRA distributions. IRA law permits participants to take distributions as early as age 59½, or sooner for specific reasons. They also are required to take distributions in a prescribed fashion once they reach age 70½.

Distributions from retirement plans may be redeposited into rollover IRAs if certain conditions are met. Properly made rollover contributions allow participants to continue to enjoy tax-deferred growth of their retirement funds. Five specific types of rollover contributions are described in this chapter.

Participants who do not follow the IRA distribution rules will be penalized by the IRS with higher taxes. IRA participants depend on financial institution employees to tell them the conditions under which allowable distributions can be taken without adverse tax consequences. Employees also need to make participants aware of those actions for which the IRS will impose penalty taxes. Since participants' distributions involve their lifetime savings, knowing the distribution rules is especially important for those institution employees who handle IRAs.

Allowable Distributions from IRAs

All IRA participants or their beneficiaries will begin receiving distributions from their IRA funds at some point in time. Withdrawals from retirement plans made or begun within a specified time period and following certain guidelines are *allowa-*

ble distributions. The general rules provide participants with flexibility as to when and how distributions can be taken. Also, IRA law provides four exceptions to participants' age restrictions for allowable distributions. This section explains the general rules, describes the participant's options and covers the four exceptions that pertain to taking allowable distributions.

General Rules

A participant between the ages of 59½ and 70½ may take allowable distributions at any time and for any amount that he or she chooses. Of course, since all money contributed into an IRA is completely and immediately vested, or nonforfeitable, the participant can withdraw it at any time. However, distributions taken before the participant is age 59½ for other than the allowable exceptions will be subject to penalty taxes.

Between the ages of 59½ and 70½ participants can take partial, also called periodic, distributions as often and for any amount that their balances will support. For example, a participant may decide to withdraw only the interest from the IRA funds. A participant also might elect to receive irregular distributions, such as $10,000 in one year and $1,000 the next. Another possibility might be for the participant to elect not to withdraw any funds at all for a given year, or until attaining a selected age between 59½ and 70½. A participant also may choose to withdraw his or her entire balance from an IRA or other retirement plan in a single payment, called a *lump-sum distribution.*

By April 1 of the calendar year following the year in which the participant reaches age 70½, the participant must begin taking distributions of a prescribed amount, known as the required minimum distribution. This means that participants who become age 70½ in 1988 will have until April 1, 1989, to either begin taking partial distributions or withdraw their entire balance.[1] The taxable year in which a participant reaches 70½ is determined from the birth date of the participant. Participants whose 70th birthdays are on or before June 30 must begin taking distributions by April 1 of the calendar year following the year in which they become 70 years old. Participants whose 70th birthdays are on or after July 1 must begin taking distributions by April 1 of the calendar year following the year in which they become age 71. For example, Andrew and Brian, twins who were born just before and just after midnight on June 30, 1927, contribute into IRAs. Assuming Andrew was born first, he will have to begin taking distributions by April 1, 1998, while his brother, Brian, can wait until April 1, 1999.

Options for Taking Distributions

Under IRA law, an IRA participant can choose from three methods of distribution. The participant may do one of the following:
- begin to receive distributions over a predetermined period of time (called a *period certain*) and according to a *payout schedule* based on life expectancy formulas. The institution would develop a payout schedule that lists the dates, frequency and amounts of periodic payments made as distributions from an IRA to the IRA participant. The participant chooses the desired timing and the institution calculates the proper amount. The IRS refers to this periodic payment option as the required minimum distribution.
- direct the trustee to purchase a single life annui-

ty or a joint life and last survivor annuity for the participant, covering the participant and spouse; or
- withdraw the entire balance in the IRA in a lump-sum distribution by April 1 following the calendar year in which he or she reaches age 70½.

If a decision regarding distribution is not made by April 1 following the calendar year in which age 70½ is reached, all of the proceeds may be distributed by the financial institution as a lump sum to be included by the participant in that year's calculation of federal income tax.

Since two of the methods of distribution (i.e., taking a lump sum or buying an annuity) are fairly straightforward, the following explanation focuses only on taking distributions over a period certain.

If a participant chooses the required minimum distribution option, the payout may be made in equal or substantially equal monthly, quarterly or annual payments. (The term "substantially equal" means no more than a minimal difference.) A participant choosing to receive minimum payments over a period certain can select either one of the following options:
- a period certain equal to or less than the participant's life expectancy; or
- a period certain equal to or less than the joint life expectancies of the participant and spouse.

Each of these options will result in minimum payments received each month, quarter or year. The financial institution is responsible for calculating the minimum payment amount.

As a result of the Tax Reform Act of 1984, an individual will be able to ask the institution annually to recalculate the minimum required distribution based on his or her then-current life expectancy. In the past, life expectancy was determined only once, at age 70½. The effect of this change is to allow a longer period of time over which funds can be distributed than was permitted before. By using annual recalculation, the maximum payment period can be expanded so that the participant can attempt to stretch out required distributions over his or her lifetime.

Life expectancy tables reflect the fact that the older a person becomes, the longer that person's expected total life span will be. In other words, the tables show that a person's remaining life expectancy decreases by less than one year for every year in age attained. The numbers in the tables are called multiples. The purpose of using the multiples is to divide the balance in a participant's account by the number of years of life expectancy. The result is the minimum required distribution. The intended effect of calculating distributions in this manner is to have participants use their IRAs for their retirement, and not as a tax-sheltered vehicle to be passed on. The higher the multiple, or longer the life expectancy, the smaller will be the fraction of the total IRA balance that must be withdrawn.

In cases where the IRA beneficiary is the participant's spouse and payments are based on joint life expectancy, joint life expectancy also may be recalculated annually. These revised IRA distribution laws became effective January 1, 1985. On July 27, 1987, the IRS issued rules that guide institutions in using these laws.

To determine the minimum amount that must be distributed under the required minimum distribution option, the trustee must divide the entire amount in the IRA at the beginning of each year after the participant reaches 70½ by the number of years of the participant's life expectancy. For example, Jack Mitchell, whose IRA was valued at $160,000 on January 1 of the year he became age 70, wishes to begin taking distributions. According to IRS actuarial tables (see Chapter 4), he is expected to live another 16 years. Therefore, his minimum distribution based on 16 years of expected additional life will be ¹⁄₁₆ of $160,000 or $10,000 to be distributed the first year. For subsequent years, the balance in his account on January 1 will be divided by his life expectancy as determined from the table. The IRS recently approved updated actuarial tables, which are based on more current mortality statistics. The new tables reflect the fact that people are now living longer than they were in the past. These updated tables allow participants to withdraw smaller amounts over a longer period of time than the tables used in the past. Since the funds in the account continue to earn interest that compounds, Jack will probably have more than $144,000 in his account by next January. The result of this yearly calculation method is that later payments could be larger than the early ones. Although the payments in later years are not equal or even approximately equal to earlier payments, such a means of distribution apparently meets the minimum distribution requirements.

A distribution schedule also may be established on a straight amortization basis, just as if the institution were repaying an installment loan to the participant. This system enables the trustee to provide equal periodic payments and still meet the minimum distribution requirements that apply for the participant.

Minimum Distribution Incidental Benefit Requirement

The Tax Reform Act of 1986 puts a limit or cap on the life expectancy multiple that may be used for determining the required minimum distribution. This limit applies to distributions from IRAs after December 31, 1988. Basically, the requirement applies in cases where a nonspouse beneficiary is named and distributions are based on the joint life expectancy of the participant and the nonspouse beneficiary. By limiting the life expectancy multiple that may be used in these cases, this rule requires distributions to be such that the participant would receive a majority of the funds in the IRA over the participant's life expectancy. The funds left to a nonspouse beneficiary are an incidental, not primary, purpose of an IRA. When a participant names a nonspouse beneficiary who is much younger, their joint life expectancy will be much longer than the participant's life expectancy. In extreme cases, if distributions were based on this multiple, the participant would not be using the IRA in the manner that the IRS had intended. The effect of the rule is to prevent participants from shifting income (and the tax liabilities) from themselves to their nonspouse beneficiaries.

Other Allowable Distributions

Four exceptions to the general rules permit distributions to be taken before age 59½ without penalty. Distributions can be taken from a participant's IRA if the participant has died, is disabled or divorced. Also, the Tax Reform Act of 1986 allows for distributions to be made before age 59½ if the participant elects to take the payments in the form of annuitized payments over the individual's life expectancy. Each of these exceptions is explained below.

Death

An IRA participant may name a beneficiary to receive the IRA funds upon his or her death. The beneficiary must be a person. An entity may not be named as a beneficiary. A single beneficiary or joint beneficiaries may be designated as well as a contingent beneficiary who receives the funds if the first-named beneficiary has predeceased the participant. If a participant dies before receiving any distributions, the entire amount of the IRA is distributed to the named beneficiary. If the participant has not named beneficiaries or if the named beneficiaries have died prior to the participant, the IRA funds become payable in a lump sum to the participant's estate.

The IRA participant may elect, from legally specified options, the manner in which death benefits are to be paid to the beneficiary. The options available to the beneficiary depend on whether the participant died before or after December 31, 1983. This holds true regardless of when the beneficiary contacts the savings institution.

Death before December 31, 1983. Beneficiaries of IRA participants who died on or before December 31, 1983, have five years to choose any of the following options:
- Receive the entire amount in a single sum. All funds can be withdrawn at any time within five years after the death of the IRA participant.
- Treat the IRA as his or her own. The beneficiary's "assumable" IRA remains subject to the same age requirements for distributions as regular IRAs. The beneficiary may elect to take this option during the five-year period following the participant's death. If the beneficiary has taken no action before the end of the five-year period,

the beneficiary will be assumed to have taken this option.
- Receive periodic payments. Periodic payments can be made to the beneficiary over a five-year period after the death of the IRA participant.
- Receive an annuity payout. Beneficiaries may choose an annuity that does not exceed their life expectancy.

If the participant has begun to receive payments from his or her IRA over a period certain and dies before the payments are completed, the beneficiary does not have a choice. In this case, the beneficiary will continue to receive payments in the same manner. The beneficiary must receive distributions at least as fast as the deceased was receiving.

Death after December 31, 1983. The Tax Equity and Fiscal Responsibility Act of 1982 changed the options available to beneficiaries after December 31, 1983. IRA beneficiaries, except surviving spouses, must receive lump-sum or periodic payment distributions within five years of the participant's death. If there are funds remaining in the IRA for more than five years, a penalty of 50% of the amount remaining in the account is charged to the beneficiary. The beneficiary may receive periodic payments over a period greater than five years, but only if period-certain payments to the IRA participant began before the death of the participant. In this case, the beneficiary must receive distributions at least as fast as the deceased was receiving. Recall that period certain payments are payments made over a specific term not exceeding the joint life expectancy of the participant and the participant's spouse.

Beneficiaries can no longer use IRA proceeds to

purchase life annuity contracts. Also, only the surviving spouse of a participant can treat the participant's IRA as his or her own. Other beneficiary relations no longer have this option. At one time, an IRA participant could leave up to $100,000 to a beneficiary without the consequence of estate taxes. That $100,000 exclusion has now been eliminated. Special transitional rules apply for participants who died prior to December 31, 1984. For a detailed analysis of beneficiaries' options regarding income and estate tax consequences, individuals should be advised to consult an attorney or reliable tax advisor.

Disability
Distributions can be taken from an IRA without penalty if a participant becomes disabled. The Internal Revenue Code defines a "disabled person" as one who "is unable to engage in any substantial gainful activity by reason of any medically determinable physical or mental impairment which can be expected to result in death or to be of long-continued and indefinite duration."[2] Disability must be certified by a licensed physician. To provide a practical basis for ascertaining when disability has occurred, IRS regulations state that disability must render the participant unable to engage in his or her "customary or any comparable substantial gainful activity."[3]

According to this definition, any disabled IRA participant can receive distributions without regard to age. The disabled participant can take any one of the three distribution options below:
- lump-sum;
- annuity; or
- period certain payments.

The participant also may take distributions on an

as-needed basis—providing that a doctor certifies that the condition will continue for a long or indefinite period, or is likely to result in death.

Divorce
Any part of the proceeds of an IRA may be transferred to an IRA in the name of a former spouse under a divorce decree or written agreement executed pursuant to a divorce. In such cases, the new IRA is considered to be maintained for the benefit of the spouse, who must follow all of the appropriate regulations regarding contributions and distributions.

Annuitized Payments Based on Life Expectancy
Beginning in 1987, a fourth exception to the general rules of prohibiting withdrawals prior to age 59½ is permitted by the Tax Reform Act of 1986. However, it is important to note that at the time of this text's printing, the IRS has yet to issue rules on this. Therefore, participants wishing to use this new exception should be referred to their tax advisors. Formerly, if funds were withdrawn before age 59½ except because of death, disability or divorce, the IRS would levy a penalty of 10% on amounts withdrawn. However, beginning in 1987, distributions may be taken from an IRA without the 10% tax penalty if payments are taken in the form of annuitized payments over the participant's life expectancy. An *annuity* is a contract between an individual and a life insurance company in which the company guarantees payment of periodic income, usually to extend over the lifetime of a person or persons. A distribution taken before age 59½ that is used to purchase an annuity is treated as a rollover contribution, which will be explained in a later section. As annuity payments are received, they are treated in the same way that other allowable distributions are treated.

Treatment of Allowable Distributions

Whenever a distribution is made, both the institution and the participant are required to report the withdrawal to the IRS. The participant is responsible for calculating any taxes that may apply. If any nondeductible contributions were made, the participant must follow special IRS-supplied instructions. To facilitate the payment of taxes, the participant may ask the institution to withhold a portion of each distribution to be submitted to the IRS. Also, whenever a distribution is made, the institution must obtain and report the reason for the withdrawal along with other specific information.

A participant who receives an IRA distribution must include this income when completing his or her federal income tax return for the year in which the distribution is received. If the participant elects a lump-sum distribution, the participant's taxes may be more severe than if the required minimum distribution is taken.

The Tax Reform Act of 1986 allows individuals age 59½ a one-time election to average a lump-sum distribution over five years. A special transitional rule also would allow this election for individuals who reach age 50 by January 1, 1986. Previously allowed 10-year averaging is repealed; pre-1974 capital gains treatment will be phased out over a six-year period.

Nondeductible Contributions as They Affect Distributions

Before 1987, all IRA contributions qualified as deductible for income tax purposes. Such distributions are then taxed as ordinary income when taken. However, beginning in 1987, certain limitations have been placed on eligibility and deductibility. For further discussion of these specifics, refer to Chapter 2.

Generally speaking, if an individual qualifies for and makes *only* deductible contributions, then distributions will be taxed as income in the year in which they are taken, as in the past. For individuals who have made *both* deductible and nondeductible contributions to an IRA, however, all future distributions will be treated as a combination of deductible contributions, nondeductible contributions and earnings. To determine the taxable portion of a distribution, it must be multiplied by an exclusion ratio.

Nondeductible contributions themselves are not taxable when withdrawn, but their earnings or gains are taxable. The exclusion ratio is a participant's total nondeductible contributions divided by the total value of all the participant's IRAs at year-end, plus distributions for the year. This fraction is then multiplied by the total amount of distributions for the year. The result is the amount of nontaxable distributions for the year.

A participant can use the formula shown in Figure 3-1 to determine the nontaxable portion of his or her distribution for a taxable year. For example, Bruce Manion makes $4,000 in nondeductible contributions over the years. Bruce then withdraws $3,000. The total value of all of his IRAs at the end of the year is $37,000. Bruce's withdrawals during the year plus the value of his IRA are equal to $37,000 plus $3,000, or $40,000. Bruce's total nondeductible contribution amount of $4,000 represents 10% of his total IRA balance (4,000/40,000). Therefore, 10% of Bruce's withdrawal of $3,000, or

$300, is his tax-free portion. The remaining 90%, or $2,700, becomes part of Bruce's taxable income.

Since all IRAs are considered as one contract, distributions will be treated as including both types of contributions, even if deductible contributions are kept in one account and nondeductible contributions are kept in a separate account. Each individual participant is responsible for designating whether a contribution is deductible or nondeductible when completing his or her federal income tax return.

Withholding

As of January 1, 1983, TEFRA requires that taxes be withheld from IRA, SEP and other plan distributions. However, participants in these plans may elect not to have amounts withheld. Institutions making distributions must notify participants of the right to make the election.

If distributions are periodic payments scheduled at least as frequently as quarterly, institutions must

---

FIGURE 3-1
Formula for Determining Nontaxable Distributions

$$\text{Nontaxable Amount} = \text{Total Distributions for the year} \times \frac{\text{Total Nondeductible Contributions}}{\text{Year-end Balance of all IRAs plus distributions for the year}}$$

notify participants of the election at least once during each calendar year. Notices must be given no earlier than six months before and no later than the date of the first payment. If distributions are less frequent than quarterly, or are nonperiodic (payable on demand), notices are given at the time of each distribution.

For scheduled periodic payments, the amount withheld is based on tables constructed by the U.S. Treasury. With nonperiodic distributions, the amount withheld is 10% of the distribution.

Distribution Statements

IRA sponsors are required to report any IRA distributions to the IRS. All distributions must be reported, even if the participant is over 59½. Also, the reason for the withdrawal must be stated on the report. The participant also must file a special tax form, reporting the distribution. Distributions must be reported, even if the individual intends to roll over the funds within 60 days.

Specific information must be reported on an individual's tax return any year a nondeductible contribution is made and any year a distribution is made from an IRA. The participant is responsible for reporting the following information:
- amount of designated nondeductible contributions for the tax year;
- total amount of nondeductible contributions for all previous years which have not been withdrawn;
- year-end total balance of all IRAs; and
- amount of distributions during the year and any other information the IRS may require.

Financial institutions will not be required to designate whether a contribution is deductible or nondeductible. That responsibility belongs to the individual participant.

Rollovers

A *rollover* occurs when a distribution from a qualified pension plan or an IRA is made to a participant who then subsequently reinvests the funds in an IRA. Distributions are a significant aspect of rollover transactions, because the rollover contribution represents all or a specific portion of a lump-sum distribution.

Rollovers provide *portability*; that is, a rollover provides a means of moving funds from a qualified pension plan to an IRA, or from one IRA to another IRA. Rollovers also are used as *conduits* to funnel retirement funds from one type of qualified pension plan to another. In these cases, participants who follow the tax law provisions are taking an allowable distribution for rollover purposes.

An *IRA transfer* differs from a rollover. To enact a transfer, the participant gives written instructions that funds be sent from the present trustee to the new trustee. Money may be transferred directly in this way as often as the participant wishes. The IRS does not consider IRA transfers to be either rollovers or distributions.[4]

To qualify as a rollover, funds from an IRA or qualified pension plan must be placed in an IRA within 60 days from the day the participant receives the distribution. In addition to this requirement, rollovers from one IRA plan to another IRA plan are restricted to a limit of one every 12 months for a participant. The 12-month period begins on the date the funds are distributed from the first IRA to the participant for rollover purposes. Thus, if a participant receives a partial or full distribution from one IRA plan on October 24 of one year, he or she may not receive another distribution from the same IRA for rollover purposes until October 24 of the next year and so on. This 12-month rule applies *only* to rollovers from one IRA plan to another; there is no limitation on rollovers from a qualified pension plan to an IRA.

Properly made rollover contributions have no immediate tax implications as to either deductions or inclusion in taxable income because such funds come from a tax-sheltered retirement plan or another IRA. Improper activity with respect to a rollover transaction is subject to the same tax penalties as regular IRAs. The same distribution rules described in this chapter for IRAs also apply to rollover transactions. Allowable distributions may be made when a participant is between the ages of 59½ and 70½, or prior to age 59½ in the case of death, disability, divorce or when taken in the form of annuitized payments based on the participant's life expectancy.

The following five types of rollovers are permitted by the Internal Revenue Code:
- rollovers that represent either a partial or lump-sum distribution to an IRA;
- rollovers from a Keogh to an IRA;
- rollovers from one retirement savings plan to another;
- rollovers from a Section 403(b) tax-sheltered annuity or custodial account to an IRA; and
- rollovers from a qualified retirement bond purchase to an IRA.

Partial Distribution Rollover to an IRA

Any time an individual receives a lump-sum or plan termination distribution from a qualified pension or retirement plan, the distribution can be tax sheltered by rolling the distribution over into an IRA within 60 days. The individual also may decide to take part of the distribution into his or her income for that year, paying income tax on it, and roll the rest into an IRA.

In the past, in order for all or any part of such assets to be rolled over into an IRA, a lump-sum distribution or plan termination had to occur all in one year. Because of changes in the law, an individual may now roll over a *partial distribution* to an IRA from a qualified plan if two conditions are met:
- the partial distribution is equal to at least 50% of the balance of the individual's credit in the plan (or tax-sheltered annuity); and
- the distribution is made because of death, disability or separation from service.

If the individual is married, spousal consent may be required to elect a distribution option other than a joint and survivor annuity (automatic annuity). A large sum of money could be involved in such a rollover. Individuals should consult a professional tax advisor both to assure that the rollover is permissible and for guidance as to the effect of such a rollover.

Employees are also allowed another rollover from a qualified pension plan to a conduit IRA. These funds remain eligible as a conduit that can be rolled into another qualified plan as long as no other IRA contributions are mixed with them. After rolling over all or any portion of the lump-sum distribution from a qualified pension plan into an IRA, an individual who becomes eligible to participate in another qualified plan can roll over the IRA funds into the new plan. For example, an employee leaves a company, receives a lump-sum distribution from the pension plan and establishes an IRA with a rollover contribution. The employee joins a new company and becomes eligible to participate in the new company's pension plan. The employee may then choose to roll over the IRA funds into the new qualified plan, providing the new plan will accept such funds.

A surviving spouse of a qualified pension plan participant can roll over all or any portion of a lump-sum distribution received on account of the participant's death. The resulting IRA must be maintained by and for the spouse, subject to the same conditions and limitations applicable to any other IRA participant. The spouse is not allowed to use the IRA as a conduit, that is, to make a subsequent rollover of the funds into his or her own qualified pension plan.

Rollover from a Keogh Plan to an IRA

A rollover from a Keogh plan to an IRA can be made either by a self-employed individual (including an owner-employee) or by a person who is employed by the self-employed individual (called a "common law" employee) or by a spouse, if the participant is deceased.

To establish an IRA with a rollover contribution, the owner-employee must either be age 59½ or disabled or must have terminated the Keogh plan. Once an owner-employee has taken a distribution from a Keogh plan and established an IRA with a rollover contribution he or she is barred for five years from making (or permitting others acting on his or her behalf from making) contributions to a Keogh plan in which he or she participates as an owner-employee. However, the five-year limitation does not apply in the case of plan termination.

Common law employees participating in a Keogh plan are eligible for rollovers only if they meet the age requirement or leave the employer, or if the employer terminates the Keogh plan or discontinues making contributions to it.

Rollover from One Retirement Savings Plan to Another

Once each year, an individual who has been making regular IRA contributions to a retirement savings plan (account, annuity or bond) can roll over all or any portion of those funds into a different retirement savings plan. Unlike rollovers of qualified plan funds, rollovers of this type have no adverse consequences due to commingling of funds. For example, a participant in a retirement annuity who rolls over his or her earnings into an IRA can contribute to that account in subsequent years. However, retirement savings plans that begin as IRAs, retirement annuities or bonds cannot be rolled over into qualified company pension plans or Keogh plans.

This type of rollover is especially useful for owners of retirement bonds, who will not earn interest on their bonds after the end of the taxable year in which they reach the age of 70½. During that year, or earlier, the participant can redeem the bonds and transfer the entire proceeds to an IRA or a retirement annuity. Thereafter, allowable distributions can begin over a fixed time period, and the retirement savings will continue to earn interest during the distribution period.

Rollover from a Section 403(b) Tax-Sheltered Annuity or Custodial Account to an IRA

For taxable years beginning after December 31, 1978, all or any part of a lump-sum distribution from a Section 403(b) tax-sheltered annuity or custodial account may be rolled over into an IRA. As with other rollovers, the general rollover requirements apply to this type of rollover. Similarly, this type of IRA rollover may be used as a conduit for subsequent rollover into another IRA or into another Section 403(b) annuity or custodial account. However, this rollover cannot be used as a conduit for subsequent rollover into a qualified pension plan. When used as a conduit, the full amount in the IRA must be distributed and all these funds must be rolled over into the successor annuity or custodial account.

Rollover from a Qualified Retirement Bond Purchase Plan to an IRA

Rollovers of bond redemption proceeds from a Section 405(a) qualified plan must be made within 60 days after the participant receives the proceeds. All or any portion of the proceeds may be included in the IRA contribution. Once established in an IRA, these funds may not be rolled over again into a qualified plan.

Penalized Distributions

To discourage the use of IRAs as a short-term means of savings, IRA law penalizes nonallowable distributions. There are three types of nonallowable distributions discussed in this section: premature distributions, underdistributions and excess distributions. Financial institution employees need to make participants aware of the additional tax consequences that will result if withdrawals other than the previously discussed allowable distributions are taken.

Premature Distributions

The Internal Revenue Service makes a distinction between three different types of premature distributions and figures the penalty differently for each. The three types of premature distributions are called actual distributions, a pledge of IRA funds and constructive distributions. The IRS assesses a 10% penalty tax in addition to any regular income taxes that may apply to premature distributions. Distributions received by a participant that are not considered premature include the following:
- those made to cure an excess contribution;
- those used to make a rollover contribution;
- those in the form of annuitized payments based on the participant's life expectancy;
- those made as a result of death or disability of the participant; or
- those made as a transfer to a spouse due to divorce.

In these five cases, no tax penalty is incurred.

Actual Distributions from an IRA

The first type of premature distribution involves an actual distribution of IRA funds to a participant who has not reached age 59½. An *actual distribution* is one in which IRA funds are, in fact, received by the participant. For example, Myra Bellington established and IRA when she was 26. At 29, when her IRA was valued at $4,800, she withdrew $3,000. Because of this premature distribution, Myra suffers several tax consequences. She must add the $3,000 to her other income for that year when computing her income taxes. In addition, Myra will probably have to pay $300 as a premature distribution penalty, or excise tax, for that year (10% of $3,000). Note that only the amount actually received is subject to the 10% tax penalty.

Pledge of IRA Funds

The second type of premature distribution (which is also considered an actual distribution) involves a *pledge* of an amount of IRA funds as security or collateral for a loan. An amount pledged is considered a premature distribution no matter what the participant's age and may be subject to the 10% tax penalty.

To understand more clearly the tax consequences of a pledge of IRA funds, consider the case of Herman Badillo. Herman had a total of $25,000 in income during the taxable year and his IRA was worth $9,000 as of September 30 of that year. On October 10 of the same year, because Herman executed a pledge giving $4,000 of his IRA to a bank as security for a personal loan, this portion of his IRA was considered distributed. Therefore, Herman's total income for the taxable year equaled $29,000 ($25,000 in income plus the $4,000 premature distribution), and the $29,000 was thus subject to ordinary income tax. Herman also had to pay a $400 penalty (10% of $4,000) on the premature distribution. Had Herman pledged the entire account for the loan, he would have had to treat his total IRA balance as being distributed.

Constructive Distribution

The third type of premature distribution involves a constructive distribution. A *constructive distribution* is one in which the IRA participant does not

receive any IRA funds directly. A constructive distribution occurs when a participant or his or her beneficiary (or other "disqualified person") commits an act which constitutes a prohibited transaction. *Prohibited transactions* are defined by the Internal Revenue Service to cover the following three actions:
- borrowing money from an IRA;
- selling property to an IRA; or
- receiving unreasonable compensation for managing an IRA.

If any of the following individuals engage in a prohibited transaction, the IRA participant is penalized:
- the participant;
- the trustee; or
- a disqualified person, including
  —anyone who exercises discretionary authority or control over the IRA;
  —a person providing services to the plan;
  —an officer, director or other person having an officer's responsibilities; and their spouses, ancestors, lineal descendants and their spouse's lineal descendants.

The Internal Revenue Service has indicated that the following conditions constitute prohibited transactions:
- sale, exchange or leasing of any property between a plan and a disqualified person;
- lending of money or extension of credit between a plan and a disqualified person;
- furnishing of goods, services or facilities between a plan and a disqualified person;
- transfer to, or use by or for, the benefit of a plan's income or assets by a disqualified person;
- dealing with a plan's income or assets by a disqualified person, acting as a fiduciary, in his

or her own interest, or for his or her own account; and
- receipt by a disqualified person, who is a fiduciary, of any personal inducement (called a consideration) from any person who will deal with a plan's income or assets.[5]

If a prohibited transaction occurs, the IRA loses its special tax status. The *total* IRA balance is treated as constructively distributed, even though the participant has not directly received any IRA funds. The total IRA balance is affected even if the prohibited transaction results in removal of only a portion of the IRA funds. The amount of the constructive distribution equals the fair market value of the IRA as of the first day of the year in which the prohibited transaction occurred. The constructive distribution must be included in gross income for that taxable year and is, therefore, subject to taxation as ordinary income. This amount is also subject to the 10% premature distribution penalty (unless the IRA participant is disabled or has attained 59½ years of age).

Underdistribution

For tax years after 1987, the IRA law requires that distributions be made in full or at least must begin by April 1 following the calendar year in which a participant reaches age 70½. Otherwise, the Internal Revenue Service may impose a 50% penalty on the *excess accumulation*—the difference between the amount that should have been distributed from the IRA and the actual amount distributed. This penalty can be imposed if a participant receives either *no* distributions or *less* than he or she was required to receive. Tax penalties also can be imposed on the beneficiaries if they have not received the total proceeds of the IRA within the time allotted for distribution.

The tax penalty on any of these underdistributions is 50% of the difference between the minimum payment required for that year and the amount actually received. However, the Revenue Act of 1978 amended the Internal Revenue Code to give the Secretary of the Treasury the authority to waive the 50% penalty for tax years 1975 and after, if the participant establishes on IRS Form 5329 that:
- the underdistribution was due to reasonable error; and
- reasonable steps are being taken to remedy the underdistribution. IRA participants who have paid the 50% penalty for previous taxable years may be able to seek tax relief by filing an amended return and establishing their eligibility for the waiver.

The tax consequences of an underdistribution can be seen in the following example. Rudi Schmidt's required distribution for the taxable year was $10,000, but he purposefully received only $6,000. Rudi was required to pay a penalty tax of 50% of the excess accumulation of $4,000 (the difference between $10,000 and $6,000) or $2,000. The $2,000 penalty was paid in addition to Rudi's other taxes on the $6,000 distribution and any other income received that year.

Excess Distributions

The IRS may impose excess distribution tax penalties in two situations. One is for excess distributions taken by the participant and the other may occur after the participant's death. The IRS will impose a 15% penalty tax in addition to any regular income tax that may apply in both situations.

Before Death
A 15% IRS excess distribution penalty tax will be imposed on any IRA distributions made after December 31, 1986, that, in the aggregate, exceed $112,500 during any calendar year. The $112,500 figure is to be indexed at the same time and in the same manner as the dollar limitation on annual benefits under a defined benefit pension plan. This penalty does not apply to distributions over the $112,500 figure pertaining to amounts distributed due to death, a qualified domestic relations order, distribution of nontaxable contributions or amounts that are rolled over within 60 days of distribution.

After Death
After a participant's death, the IRS can impose an excess retirement accumulation tax of 15%. The *excess retirement accumulation* can be subject to a one-time federal estate tax penalty. It is levied against an estate if an individual's total interest in qualified retirement plans, tax-sheltered annuities and IRAs exceeds the present value of an annuity with annual payments of $112,500 or 125% of the limitation for defined benefit plans in effect for the year. Annuity value is calculated using the individual's life expectancy just before death. For example, if the person died at age 72, then the annuity value used would be the life expectancy of a 72-year-old.

Following is an example illustrating the 15% excess retirement accumulation tax. An individual dies leaving account balances that would purchase a 10-year annuity of $132,500. In this case, the excess accumulation would be equal to $132,500 minus

$112,500, or $20,000. The excess accumulation tax would then be calculated as 15% on the excess, or $20,000 X .15 = $3,000. This tax is a one-time penalty.

Summary

Recent changes in IRA law generally affect distributions in a number of ways: through liberalization of exceptions that allow distributions to be received before 59½ without penalty and through the establishment of nondeductible IRA contributions. Figure 3-2 summarizes and compares these changes with the previous laws. Distributions usually will not begin until the participant reaches age 59½. Allowable exceptions include cases of death, disability, divorce or annuitized payments based on life expectancy. An IRA participant must begin taking distributions using one of three distribution options (lump-sum, annuity or period certain payments) by April 1 following the calendar year in which the participant reaches age 70½.

A significant aspect of rollovers is that a rollover contribution is made with a lump-sum distribution from a qualified pension plan. Rollovers incur no tax liability for the participant. Rollovers are allowed in five instances:
- from a qualified pension plan to an IRA;
- from a Keogh plan to an IRA;
- from one retirement savings plan to another;
- from a Section 403(b) tax-sheltered annuity/custodial account to an IRA; and
- from a qualified retirement bond purchase plan to an IRA.

Partial distribution rollovers from qualified plans to IRAs are now allowed if a rollover is equal to at least 50% of the balance of the individual's credit in

FIGURE 3-2
Summary and Comparison of Current and Old Laws as They Affect Distributions

Tax Reform Changes

- Individuals may take allowable distributions from an IRA prior to age 59½ if withdrawals are taken in the form of annuitized payments based on the participant's life expectancy.

- Guidelines for the establishment of nondeductible IRAs have been established. Distributions for participants who have made both deductible and nondeductible contributions will be treated as a combination of both types of funds, even if kept in separate accounts. All IRA accounts for a participant will be treated as one IRA contract.

- The deadline for taking required minimum distributions for the years 1985 and 1986 has been extended to December 31, 1987. This is an extension only, not a change in the law. Normally, required minimum distributions must begin by April 1 following the year in which the participant turns 70½.

- For the purposes of determining distributions, life expectancy may now be recalculated every year.

- Rules relating to rolling over lump-sum or plan termination distributions from qualified plans to IRAs have been expanded. An individual may now roll over funds into an IRA from a qualified plan if the funds are equal to at least 50% of the balance of the individual's credit in the plan, and the rollover is made because of death, disability or separation from service.

Old Law

- The only reasons for allowable distribution were because of death, disability or divorce.

- All IRA contributions were deductible.

- Distributions were required by the end of the year in which the participant turns 70½.

- Life expectancy was determined only once, at age 70½.

- In order for all or any part of such assets to be rolled over into an IRA, a lump-sum distribution or plan termination had to occur all in one year.

the plan and if it is made because of death, disability or separation from service.

Distributions taken before age 59½ are considered premature and are subject to a 10% penalty. Other prohibited actions, such as using IRA funds as collateral, also could trigger the 10% penalty. If a participant who is over age 70½ does not receive the minimum amount from the IRA, an underdistribution results. Underdistributions are subject to a 50% penalty on the excess accumulation (the difference between the amount the participant should have received and the amount, in fact, received). Also, if a very large amount is distributed in one year or bequeathed, the IRS may impose a 15% excess distribution tax.

Chapter Questions

1. Under most circumstances, what would be the earliest age at which allowable distributions would begin? At what age *must* distributions begin?
2. Under what circumstances may IRA distributions be taken before the participant reaches the minimum required age?
3. What three options may a participant choose for taking an allowed distribution?
4. What effect will nondeductible contributions to IRAs have on future distributions?
5. What is the time limit for establishing an IRA by rolling over a lump-sum distribution?
6. Under what circumstances is a partial distribution rollover to an IRA allowed? What percentage must be rolled over into an IRA?
7. Name five types of rollovers and outline specific requirements for each of them.
8. What is the tax penalty for premature distributions? What are the tax consequences?
9. What are the three types of premature distributions?
10. What is the difference between actual distribution and constructive distribution?
11. What is the tax penalty for underdistribution? What are the tax consequences of underdistribution?

Footnotes

[1]IRC, Section 401(a)(9). Because of recent tax reform, however, the deadline for taking the required minimum distributions for the years 1985 and 1986 has been extended to December 31, 1987. This includes participants who turn 70½ during those years. The 1987 required minimum distribu-

tion for those turning 70½ before 1987 *also* must be taken by December 31, 1987. Those reaching 70½ during 1987 must take the required minimum distribution by April 1, 1988.

It is particularly important for IRA participants nearing 70½, and those over that age, to consult both with their IRA sponsors and with a reliable tax advisor to insure that they meet and follow the minimum distribution requirements.

[2] IRC, Section 72(m)(7) and Title 26 of the U.S. Code, Section 72(m)(7).

[3] Title 26 of the Code of Federal Regulations, Section 1.72-17(f).

[4] IRS, Revenue Ruling 78-406.

[5] IRC, Section 4975(c) for prohibited transactions and Section 4975(d) for exemptions.

Opening and Servicing IRAs

Chapter Four

Chapter Four
Objectives

After studying this chapter, you should be able to:
- Identify situations in which a financial institution can be held legally liable for breach of fiduciary responsibility;
- List some basic provisions of an IRA trust account agreement;
- Identify the required forms for opening an IRA;
- Explain the purposes of the disclosure statement; and
- Describe how IRA trustees carry out five major administrative activities they are responsible for after an IRA is established.

THIS CHAPTER covers the basics of offering, opening and maintaining IRAs. It explains the role that an institution assumes when it provides IRAs. As a trustee for the IRA participant, the institution agrees to assume fiduciary responsibilities. The documents used to open an IRA spell out both the trustee's and the participant's responsibilities. To better serve their customers, institution employees need to know not only how to properly complete the forms used to open an IRA, but also the significance of the information that must be reported. Once the IRA is established, the institution must report certain information to the IRA participants and to the IRS and Social Security Administration by specific dates.

Offering IRA Programs

Before offering IRAs to the public, most financial institutions will implement a broad range of carefully considered plans. Employees will be instructed on the proper way to carry out the institution's fiduciary responsibilities to the participants. These responsibilities are listed in the trust account agreement, which employees should be able to explain to customers. Many institutions also train their employees in how most effectively to communicate the terms and conditions of the available investment options provided for IRAs.

Fiduciary Responsibility

By offering an IRA program, a financial institution enters into a fiduciary relationship with the IRA participant. A *fiduciary* is a person or corporation with the responsibility of holding or controlling property for another. In this relationship, the institution serves as trustee of the funds deposited by the participant, who is also known as the grantor. As mentioned in Chapter 2, the trustee exercises discretionary control or authority over the IRA assets and must meet the legal standards of reasonable care, skill, prudence and diligence in the administration of the IRA funds.

As a fiduciary, the financial institution must be prepared to guard against the possibility of legal action. Legal action can arise from three sources: the account holder, state and federal regulators of financial institutions, and the IRS.

- An account holder may attempt to prove that he or she suffered adverse consequences as a result of the institution's acting negligently, failing to follow its contract, or giving legal, tax law or investment advice. Legally an institution may be held liable for negligence if it:
  —fails to keep accurate track of balances due individual participants;
  —pays benefits to the wrong beneficiaries (for example, to a contingent beneficiary instead of to a primary beneficiary); or
  —pays an incorrect amount to a proper beneficiary.
- State and federal regulators may impose fines and other sanctions upon the institution for not complying with regulations in situations such as the following:
  —making imprudent or not permitted investment decisions; or
  —failing to obtain a death certificate before paying out to a beneficiary.
- The IRS may fine the institution if it fails to:
  —file required reports and/or tax data by specific due dates;
  —provide the participant with required reports, copies, disclosures and notices;
  —keep accurate records necessary for reporting; or

—properly withhold federal income tax on IRA withdrawals.[1]

As trustee, the financial institution may rely on information submitted by the participant, including the amount of IRA contributions made during each taxable year. Although the institution is not required to monitor whether any contribution is within a participant's percentage limitation for yearly contributions, the institution cannot accept contributions in excess of the dollar limitations for any particular type of IRA. Recall that an IRA may be opened and funded with several kinds of contributions, namely, regular, spousal, direct transfer, rollover and SEP contributions.

Trust Account Agreement

Financial institutions must adopt a trust account agreement before offering IRAs. A *trust account agreement* is a contract between the institution, as trustee (or custodian), and the IRA participant as grantor. The *trustee* is the legal title holder and controller of funds in a trust account established for the benefit of another, according to a trust agreement. The agreement also may name beneficiaries of the IRA trust.

The Internal Revenue Service has issued two prototype trust account agreements—Form 5305 for trusteed plans and Form 5305-A for custodial plans. A financial institution has three options regarding IRA trust agreements:
- It may use either of the IRS forms.
- It may prepare its own trust account agreement, which the Internal Revenue Service examines and approves if it fulfills the statutory and regulatory requirements.

- It may adopt any other agreement that has already been approved by the Internal Revenue Service; this is called a "prototype plan."

Some basic provisions that a trust account agreement must include are as follows:
- The participant's interest in the account's balance is nonforfeitable;
- The participant agrees to provide information so that the trustee may prepare required reports; and
- The trustee agrees to submit reports to the Internal Revenue Service and to the participant.[2]

Terms and Conditions

After the trust account agreement has been adopted, the institution then adopts a written statement clarifying the specific terms and conditions of the savings programs it offers as repositories for IRA contributions. Retirement savings repositories at a savings institution may include any regular deposit account or certificate of deposit of that institution. Some institutions also provide self-directed IRAs. With a self-directed IRA, the participant can direct the institution to purchase a variety of non-FSLIC insured investments from outside the institution on his or her behalf.

Because a financial institution is both a depository and a trustee for IRA funds, the rules for an IRA account may include special terms and conditions such as the following:
- interest rates, whether the rates are fixed or variable and, if variable, the index or schedule that is used to determine the rate;
- provision for accumulating contributions at the regular account rate with an automatic transfer

to a certificate of deposit when the certificate minimum has been accumulated;
- provision to allow additional deposits without extending the maturity;
- provision for the participant to instruct the institution not to transfer funds or to invest funds in certain ways;
- provision to allow the institution to withdraw funds and transfer them into another account classification for better internal liquidity management;
- waiver of premature distribution penalties for early withdrawal of funds in certificates of deposit when the participant attains the retirement age, or in case of disability or death; and
- no payment of interest if the account is revoked within seven days after it is opened.

Institutions include these special IRA account terms and conditions for two main reasons: these terms give the institution flexibility in the management of funds to provide attractive interest rates; and these terms may provide flexibility to the participant making contributions and requesting distributions allowed by the IRA law.

Opening IRAs

When a new accounts counselor or other designated employee opens an IRA, four basic steps are routinely followed:
1. introduce IRAs to the prospective participant;
2. describe IRA deposit options;
3. execute documents; and
4. conduct follow-up programs.

These four steps are briefly explained below. However, individual institutions, due to specific policies and needs, may require additional procedures.

Introduce IRAs to the Prospective Participant

Prospective IRA participants have diverse backgrounds and needs. Some may not be well informed about IRAs in general or about the financial institution's account program in particular. For these reasons, institution sales representatives must tailor their introductory presentation to fit each individual's needs and knowledge.

Some institutions view IRAs as a specific type of deposit account, and see the new accounts counselor's role as that of facilitating the account opening procedures. Other institutions have adopted the concept of a financial counseling center, in which new accounts employees function as personal money management counselors. First these counselors introduce IRAs as one of many services offered by the institution to help customers manage their personal finances. Then the counselor specifically introduces IRAs as a part of the customer's total money management and retirement planning program.

An IRA counselor's typical approach is to explain the purpose of an IRA and the tax benefits an IRA offers. A counselor should stress that investing in an IRA requires careful consideration, especially for younger people, because a long-term commitment of funds is necessary to benefit fully from the IRA's tax advantages. The counselor also should describe the IRA penalties for premature distributions and their tax implications (see Chapter 3). A counselor's goal at this introductory stage is to provide information that both emphasizes the attractiveness of IRAs and makes the customer aware of the restrictions.

If the participant expresses interest in an IRA, the counselor may go on to explain the composition and limits for IRA contributions. It is the participant's responsibility, and not that of the financial institution, to make sure that he or she meets the age and compensation eligibility requirements for making IRA contributions. It also is the participant's responsibility to determine and keep track of deductible and nondeductible contributions. As Chapter 2 explained, helpful information about deductibility may be given to participants. However, the institution's employees cannot determine the actual amount of an individual's deductibility. If this information is requested, the proper response is to politely explain the following:
- Deductibility is determined at the time the participant's federal income tax return is completed.
- The IRS provides instructions on Form 1040 for determining and keeping track of deductible and nondeductible contributions.
- Institution employees are not permitted to complete a customer's tax return or otherwise render tax advice.

When opening and administering IRAs, personnel should not give legal advice to participants because such advice can subsequently lead to legal liability for the institution. Employees can supply general IRA information and answer general questions about the IRA law, but they should not answer questions pertaining to a participant's own specific problems, circumstances or personal tax consequences. For this information, a participant needs to consult qualified tax professionals and the Internal Revenue Service.

Describe IRA Deposit Options

The second step in opening an IRA is to describe the features of each of the IRA deposit options an institution offers so that the participant may make an educated choice among the options. If payroll deduction plans or other types of automatic savings plans are available for IRAs, the counselor should describe them and help the participant decide if such a plan meets his or her special needs. When describing certificates, the counselor should state the current rate of interest, explain how it is calculated, explain whether the rate of interest is fixed or variable and, if a variable rate is used, describe the index or schedule on which the rate is based, the frequency of the rate change and any limits to the rate change.

Execute Documents

After the participant has decided on a particular IRA deposit option, an IRA can be opened. The counselor completes the required documents, indicates to the participant where to sign and furnishes the participant with copies. The following four documents must be prepared:
- trust account agreement, also called the plan agreement;
- disclosure statement;
- designation of beneficiary; and
- deposit information.

Plan Agreement

As stated earlier, the plan agreement, or trust account agreement, names the financial institution as trustee (or custodian) of the funds and the participant as grantor. The agreement details the fiduciary relationship between the institution and participant and may contain all of the terms and conditions of the IRA.

The trust agreement document is completed by the IRA counselor and signed by both the participant and an officer or other authorized employee of the institution. Some state laws require that a witness also sign the agreement. The participant receives a copy, and one copy is retained by the institution. The institution also should retain verification that the account holder has been provided with a copy of the plan agreement.

The plan agreement must be current when the IRA is opened. For those institutions using Form 5305 or Form 5305-A, the current forms were revised as of November, 1983. Figure 4-1 shows the Internal Revenue Service's IRA Form 5305 trust account agreement for a trusteed IRA plan. A copy of the custodial IRA trust account agreement, Form 5305-A, is shown in Figure 4-2.

Once the IRA is established, the trustee or custodian must give account holders amendments that reflect any changes in the law that occurred after the original plan was created. The exact wording of the plan agreement can vary among institutions depending upon the type of plan that has been adopted (trustee or custodial) and whether the institution uses its own approved plan or other prototype (preapproved) plan. A separate trust account agreement is used for a SEP; this is shown in Chapter 5.

Essentially, the plan agreement contains nine articles which are summarized below.

Article I discusses the contribution limits. Currently, it states that no more than $2,000 may be accepted as a regular contribution for any tax year and that contributions must be in cash.

Article II states that the IRA account holder's balance cannot be forfeited.

Article III spells out the restrictions on IRA investments. It states that IRA funds may not be invested in life insurance contracts, or commingled with other property, except in a common trust fund or investment fund. Also, IRA funds may not be invested in collectibles, such as art, antiques or rare wines.

Articles IV and V explain the distribution rules that must be followed. They state the conditions under which allowable distributions can be made, and when and how required distributions should be made. The rules also require the account holder to furnish the institution with an explanation of what will be done with distributions that appear to be neither allowable nor required.

Article VI states both the account holder's and the institution's responsibilities. The account holder agrees to provide accurate information to the financial institution. The institution agrees to submit required IRS reports and to make sure all IRA contract provisions are consistent with IRA law.

Articles VII and VIII basically say that the IRA plan agreement will be amended as needed to comply with law changes.

Article IX allows the institution to add other provisions as long as they comply with IRA law. It also describes the institution's fiduciary responsibilities.

FIGURE 4-1
Form 5305, Side 1

Form 5305
(Rev. November, 1983)
Department of the Treasury
Internal Revenue Service

Individual Retirement Trust Account
(Under Section 408(a) of the Internal Revenue Code)

OMB No. 1545-0365

Do NOT File with Internal Revenue Service

The Grantor who completes and signs an application incorporating this agreement by reference is establishing an individual retirement account (under section 408(a) of the Internal Revenue Code) to provide for his or her retirement and for the support of his or her beneficiaries after death.
The Trustee named in the application has given the Grantor the disclosure statement required under the Income Tax Regulations under section 408 (i) of the Code.
The Grantor and the Trustee make the following agreement:

Article I
The Trustee may accept additional cash contributions on behalf of the Grantor for a tax year of the Grantor. The total cash contributions are limited to $2,000 for the tax year unless the contribution is a rollover contribution described in section 402(a)(5), 402(a)(7), 403(a)(4), 403(b)(8), 405(d)(3), 408(d)(3), or 409(b)(3)(C) of the Code or an employer contribution to a simplified employee pension plan as described in section 408(k).

Article II
The Grantor's interest in the balance in the trust account is nonforfeitable.

Article III
1. No part of the trust funds may be invested in life insurance contracts, nor may the assets of the trust account be commingled with other property except in a common trust fund or common investment fund (within the meaning of section 408(a)(5) of the Code).
2. No part of the trust funds may be invested in collectibles (within the meaning of section 408(m) of the Code).

Article IV
1. The Grantor's entire interest in the trust account must be, or begin to be, distributed before the end of the tax year in which the Grantor reaches age 70½. By the end of that year, the Grantor may elect, in a manner acceptable to the Trustee, to have the balance in the trust account distributed in:
   (a) A single sum payment.
   (b) An annuity contract that provides equal or substantially equal monthly, quarterly, or annual payments over the life of the Grantor. The payments must begin by the end of that tax year.
   (c) An annuity contract that provides equal or substantially equal monthly, quarterly, or annual payments over the joint and last survivor lives of the Grantor and his or her spouse. The payments must begin by the end of the tax year.
   (d) Equal or substantially equal monthly, quarterly, or annual payments over a specified period that may not be longer than the Grantor's life expectancy.
   (e) Equal or substantially equal monthly, quarterly, or annual payments over a specified period that may not be longer than the joint life and last survivor expectancy of the Grantor and his or her spouse.

Even if distributions have begun to be made under option (d) or (e), the Grantor may receive a distribution of the balance in the trust account at any time by giving written notice to the Trustee. If the Grantor does not choose any of the methods of distribution described above by the end of the tax year in which he or she reaches age 70½, distribution to the Grantor will be made before the end of that tax year by a single sum payment. If the Grantor elects as a means of distribution (b) or (c) above, the annuity contract must satisfy the requirements of section 408(b)(1), (3), (4), and (5) of the Code. If the Grantor elects as a means of distribution (d) or (e) above, figure the payments made in tax years beginning in the tax year the Grantor reaches age 70½ as follows:
   (i) For the minimum annual payment, divide the Grantor's entire interest in the trust account at the beginning of each year by the life expectancy of the Grantor (or the joint life and last survivor expectancy of the Grantor and his or her spouse, or the period specified under (d) or (e) whichever applies). Determine the life expectancy in either case on the date the Grantor reaches age 70½ minus the number of whole years passed since the Grantor became 70½.
   (ii) For the minimum monthly payment, divide the result in (i) above by 12.
   (iii) For the minimum quarterly payment, divide the result in (i) above by 4.
2. If the Grantor dies before his or her entire interest in the account is distributed to him or her, or if distribution is being made as provided in (e) above to his or her surviving spouse, and the surviving spouse dies before the entire interest is distributed, the entire remaining undistributed interest will, within 5 years after the Grantor's death or the death of the surviving spouse, be distributed to the beneficiary or beneficiaries of the Grantor or the Grantor's surviving spouse. However, the preceding distribution is not required if distributions over a specified term began before the death of the Grantor and the term is for a period permitted under (d) or (e) above and distributions continue over that period.
If the Grantor dies before his or her entire interest has been distributed and if the beneficiary is other than the surviving spouse, no additional cash contributions or rollover contributions may be accepted in the account.

Article V
Unless the Grantor dies, is disabled (as defined in section 72(m) of the Code), or reaches age 59½ before any amount is distributed from the trust account, the Trustee must receive from the Grantor a statement explaining how he or she intends to dispose of the amount distributed.

Article VI
1. The Grantor agrees to provide the Trustee with information necessary for the Trustee to prepare any reports required under section 408(i) of the Code and the related regulations.
2. The Trustee agrees to submit reports to the Internal Revenue Service and the Grantor as prescribed by the Internal Revenue Service.

Article VII
Notwithstanding any other articles which may be added or incorporated, the provisions of Articles I through III and this sentence will be controlling. Any additional articles that are not consistent with section 408(a) of the Code and related regulations will be invalid.

Article VIII
This agreement will be amended from time to time to comply with the provisions of the Code and related regulations. Other amendments may be made with the consent of the persons whose signatures appear below.

Article IX
1. **Definitions.**
   (a) **Grantor:** The individual who establishes an individual retirement trust account by executing this agreement, also referred to as the "Participant" in the IRA disclosure statement which is issued in connection with this agreement.
   (b) **Beneficiary:** A person or entity (including but not limited to the Grantor's (or spouse's) estate, dependent or dependents), designated in writing by the Grantor (or surviving spouse) to receive benefits payable under this agreement, subsequent to the death of the Grantor (or surviving spouse).
   (c) **Trustee:** Institution named in application as trustee.
2. **Investment Authority. (Investment Direction by Grantor.)**
   (a) At the direction of the Grantor given in the form and manner prescribed by the Trustee, the Trustee may invest in such certificates of deposit or other savings instruments as are chosen by the Grantor from among deposits designated from time to time by the Institution to be within the class or classes of deposits offered for the investment of IRA funds. If such deposits are not automatically renewable, or if the Grantor fails to give appropriate directions for investment, the funds shall be invested by the Trustee in deposits paying the then current annual

Form 5305, Side 2

rate of interest being paid by the Institution on regular deposit accounts. A class may be established in the form of a common trust fund or common investment fund as described in Article III. If authorized by law and duly licensed by proper authority, the Trustee may invest and reinvest any part of the IRA trust assets in such other investments as the Grantor may specify by appropriate directions submitted to the Trustee.

(b) The Trustee may hold a reasonable portion of the trust account in cash, with no obligation for payment of interest, for payment of current expenses or benefits under this Agreement.

3. Judicial Settlement of Accounts.

The Trustee shall have the right to apply at any time to a court of competent jurisdiction for the judicial settlement of its accounts. In any such judicial action or proceeding it shall be necessary to join as parties the Trustee and the Grantor, (or Beneficiary if Grantor is deceased). Any judgment or decree entered thereon shall be conclusive upon all persons claiming any interest in the trust account.

4. Expenses and Compensation.

The Trustee may charge against and deduct from the trust account, or receive directly from the Grantor, reimbursement for all reasonable expenses incurred by the Trustee in the administration of this trust, including costs of fiduciary insurance, counsel fees and reasonable compensation for its services as Trustee hereunder; the latter to be determined by a fee schedule set out in the IRA disclosure statement.

5. Fiduciary Responsibilities.

(a) The Trustee shall be responsible for the administration of the trust, shall receive all contributions, shall invest the trust assets pursuant to appropriate direction of the Grantor and shall make distributions and pay benefits from the trust account, shall file such statements or reports as may be required by Trustees by law, and shall do such other things as may be required in the administration of the trust. Unless otherwise directed in writing by the grantor, his spouse or beneficiaries, the Trustee in its sole discretion from time to time shall cast any votes on any and all matters, or appoint any proxy to cast such votes as may be attributable to the Grantor's interest under this agreement. The Trustee shall use reasonable care, skill, prudence and diligence in the administration of the trust and in executing the Grantor's instructions as to the investment of the trust assets and shall be entitled to rely on information submitted by the Grantor to the Trustee.

(b) The Institution shall have no duties under this agreement and no responsibility for the administration of the trust except for such duties imposed by law or this agreement on savings institutions which sponsor IRA programs. The Trustee shall have no liability regarding investments made at the direction of the Grantor other than to carry out the duties imposed under this Article.

(c) The United States League of Savings Institutions shall have no duties with respect to, or responsibility or discretionary control over the administration of the trust established pursuant to this agreement, except that it may, from time to time, make amendments to the trust agreement consistent with Section 408 of the Code or other applicable law, regulations or administrative rulings, and with paragraph 7 hereof.

6. Resignation, Removal and Appointment of Trustee.

The Trustee acting hereunder may resign at any time by giving 60 days prior written notice of such resignation to the Institution and the Grantor (or Beneficiary if Grantor is deceased). The Institution may remove any Trustee acting hereunder at any time by giving 60 days prior written notice thereof to such Trustee. The Institution shall fill any vacancy in the office of Trustee by written instrument appointing a successor Trustee, provided, however, that any successor Trustee so appointed shall be a savings and loan association, bank or trust company authorized to act as Trustee of trusts established under individual retirement accounts, organized under the laws of the United States or any State of the United States, and subject to supervision and examination by governmental authority.

7. Amendments.

This Trust agreement is intended to be and to remain a qualified individual retirement trust account within the meaning of Section 408 of the Code. For the sole purposes of insuring the continued compliance of this agreement with the requirements of applicable law, or of conforming it to statutory or regulatory changes in allowable contribution limits, this agreement may be amended unilaterally from time to time, pursuant to the first sentence of Article VIII, by the United States League of Savings Institutions by written instrument delivered to the Trustee. The United States League, pursuant to the second sentence of Article VIII, also may make such other amendments to this agreement from time to time as may be consistent with the provisions of applicable law, which amendments shall not be effective until the Trustee and the Grantor have consented thereto. No amendment to this agreement shall vest any right or interest in the trust account in any party other than the Grantor, his spouse or beneficiaries. Any amendments to this agreement pursuant to this paragraph may be effective retroactively, provided that no amendment made pursuant to the second sentence of Article VIII shall deprive the Grantor, his spouse or beneficiary of any benefit to which each may have been entitled as a result of contributions made prior to the amendment.

8. Records and Reports.

The Trustee shall maintain appropriate records for the individual retirement account showing all contributions, disbursements and investments of trust account funds which shall be open for inspection by the Grantor (or Beneficiary if Grantor is deceased) during business hours of the Trustee. In addition to the reports by Trustee required under Article VI, the Trustee shall arrange for such reports and information to be provided to the Grantor regarding the investment of the IRA funds as may reasonably be necessary to enable the Grantor to direct the investment and reinvestment of his IRA funds.

Instructions

(Section references are to the Internal Revenue Code unless otherwise noted.)

Paperwork Reduction Act Notice. — The Paperwork Reduction Act of 1980 says that we must tell you why we are collecting this information, how it is to be used, and whether you have to give it to us. The information is used to determine if you are entitled to a deduction for contributions to this trust. Your completing this information is only required if you want a qualified individual retirement account.

Purpose of Form

This model trust may be used by an individual who wishes to adopt an individual retirement account under section 408(a). When fully executed by the Grantor and the Trustee not later than the time prescribed by law for filing the Federal income tax return for the Grantor's tax year (including any extensions thereof), an individual will have an individual retirement account (IRA) trust which meets the requirements of section 408(a). This trust must be created in the United States for the exclusive benefit of the Grantor or his/her beneficiaries.

Definitions

Trustee. — The trustee must be a bank or savings and loan association, as defined in section 408(n), or other person who has the approval of the Internal Revenue Service to act as trustee.

Grantor. — The grantor is the person who establishes the trust account.

IRA for Non-Working Spouse

Contributions to an IRA trust account for a non-working spouse must be made to a separate IRA trust account established for the non-working spouse.

This form may be used to establish the IRA trust for the non-working spouse.

An employee's social security number will serve as the identification number of his or her individual retirement account. An employer identification number is not required for each individual retirement account, nor for a common fund created for individual retirement accounts.

For more information, get a copy of the required disclosure statement from your trustee or get **Publication 590**, Individual Retirement Arrangements (IRA's).

Specific Instructions

Article IV. — Distributions made under this Article may be made in a single sum, periodic payment, or a combination of both. The distribution option should be reviewed in the year the Grantor reaches age 70½ to make sure the requirements of section 408(a)(6) have been met. For example if a Grantor elects distributions over a period permitted in (d) or (e) of Article IV, the period may not extend beyond the life expectancy of the Grantor at age 70½ (under option (d)) or the joint life and last survivor expectancy of the Grantor (at age 70½) and the Grantor's spouse (under option (e)). For this purpose, life expectancies must be determined by using the expected return multiples in section 1.72-9 of the Income Tax Regulations (26 CFR Part 1). The balance in the account as of the beginning of each tax year beginning on or after the Grantor reaches age 70½ will be used in computing the payments described in (d) and (e) of Article IV. Article IV does not preclude a mode of distribution different from those described in (a) through (e) of Article IV prior to the close of the tax year of the Grantor in which he/she reaches age 70½.

Article IX. — This Article and any that follow it may incorporate additional provisions that are agreed upon by the grantor and trustee to complete the agreement. These may include, for example, definitions, investment powers, voting rights, exculpatory provisions, amendment and termination, removal of trustee, trustee's fees, State law requirements, beginning date of distributions, accepting only cash, treatment of excess contributions, prohibited transactions with the grantor, etc. Use additional pages if necessary and attach them to this form.

Certain portions of this form are taken from a U.S. Government work.

© 1984 United States League of Savings Institutions

FIGURE 4-2
Form 5305-A, Side 1

Individual Retirement Custodial Account
Form 5305-A Under Section 408(a) of the Internal Revenue Code

Do Not File With Internal Revenue Service

OMB NO. 1545-0365
FORM (REV. NOV. 1983)
DEPARTMENT OF TREASURY
INTERNAL REVENUE SERVICE

The Depositor whose name appears on the Application on the reverse side is establishing an Individual Retirement Account (under Section 408(a) of the Internal Revenue Code) to provide for his or her retirement and for the support of his or her beneficiaries after death.

The Custodian named on the Application has given the Depositor the disclosure statement required under the Income Tax Regulations under Section 408(i) of the Code.

The Depositor has deposited with the Custodian the sum indicated on the Application in cash.

The Depositor and the Custodian make the following Agreement:

ARTICLE I — The Custodian may accept additional cash contributions on behalf of the Depositor for a tax year of the Depositor. The additional cash contributions are limited to $2,000 for the tax year unless the contribution is a rollover contribution described in Section 402(a)(5), 402(a)(7), 403(a)(4), 403(b)(8), 405(d)(3), 408(d)(3), or 409(b)(3)(C) of the Code or an employer contribution to a Simplified Employee Pension Plan as described in Section 408(k).

ARTICLE II — The Depositor's interest in the balance in the Custodial account is nonforfeitable.

ARTICLE III — 1. No part of the Custodial funds may be invested in life insurance contracts, nor may the assets of the Custodial account be commingled with other property except in a common Custodial fund or common investment fund (within the meaning of Section 408(a)(5) of the Code). 2. No part of the Custodial funds may be invested in collectibles (within the meaning of Section 408(m) of the Code).

ARTICLE IV — 1. The Depositor's entire interest in the Custodial account must be, or begin to be, distributed before the end of the tax year in which the Depositor reaches age 70½. By the end of that tax year, the Depositor may elect, in a manner acceptable to the Custodian, to have the balance in the Custodial account distributed in:
(a) A single-sum payment.
(b) An annuity contract that provides equal or substantially equal monthly, quarterly, or annual payments over the life of the Depositor. The payments must begin by the end of that tax year.
(c) An annuity contract that provides equal or substantially equal monthly, quarterly, or annual payments over the joint and last survivor lives of the Depositor and his or her spouse. The payments must begin by the end of that tax year.
(d) Equal or substantially equal monthly, quarterly, or annual payments over a specified period that may not be longer than the Depositor's life expectancy.
(e) Equal or substantially equal monthly, quarterly, or annual payments over a specified period that may not be longer than the joint life and last survivor expectancy of the Depositor and his or her spouse.

Even if distributions have begun to be made under option (d) or (e), the Depositor may receive a distribution of the balance in the Custodial account at any time by giving written notice to the Custodian. If the Depositor does not choose any of the methods of distribution described above by the end of the tax year in which he or she reaches age 70½, distribution to the Depositor will be made before the end of that tax year by a single-sum payment. If the Depositor elects as a means of distribution (b) or (c) above, the annuity contract must satisfy the requirements of Section 408(b)(1), (3), (4), and (5) of the Code. If the Depositor elects as a means of distribution (d) or (e) above, figure the payments made in tax years beginning in the tax year the Depositor reaches age 70½ as follows:
(i) For the minimum annual payment, divide the Depositor's entire interest in the Custodial account at the beginning of each year by the life expectancy of the Depositor [or the joint life and last survivor expectancy of the Depositor and his or her spouse, or the period specified under (d) or (e), whichever applies]. Determine the life expectancy in either case on the date the Depositor reaches 70½ minus the number of whole years passed since the Depositor became 70½.
(ii) For the minimum monthly payment, divide the result in (i) above by twelve.
(iii) For the minimum quarterly payment, divide the result in (i) above by four.

2. If the Depositor dies before his or her entire interest in the account is distributed to him or her, or if distribution is being made as provided in (e) above to his or her surviving spouse, and the surviving spouse dies before the entire interest is distributed, the entire remaining undistributed interest will, within five years after the Depositor's death or the death of the surviving spouse, be distributed to the beneficiary or beneficiaries of the Depositor or the Depositor's surviving spouse. However, the preceding distribution is not required if distributions over a specified term began before the death of the Depositor and the term is for a period permitted under (d) or (e) above and distributions continue over that period.
If the Depositor dies before his or her entire interest has been distributed, and if the beneficiary is other than the surviving spouse, no additional cash contributions or rollover contributions may be accepted in the account.

ARTICLE V — Unless the Depositor dies, is disabled (as defined in Section 72(m) of the Code), or reaches age 59½ before any amount is distributed from the account, the Custodian must receive from the Depositor a statement explaining how he or she intends to dispose of the amount distributed.

ARTICLE VI — 1. The Depositor agrees to provide the Custodian with information necessary for the Custodian to prepare any reports required under Section 408(i) of the Code and the related regulations. 2. The Custodian agrees to submit reports to the Internal Revenue Service and the Depositor as prescribed by the Internal Revenue Service.

ARTICLE VII — Notwithstanding any other articles which may be added or incorporated, the provisions of Articles I through III and this sentence will be controlling. Any additional articles that are not consistent with Section 408(a) of the Code and related regulations will be invalid.

ARTICLE VIII — This Agreement will be amended from time to time to comply with the provisions of the Code and related regulations. Other amendments may be made with the consent of the persons whose signatures appear below.

CONTINUED

Form 5305-A, Side 2

ARTICLE IX

Definitions: In this part of this Agreement (Article IX), the words "you" and "your" mean the Depositor and the words "we," "us" and "our" mean the Custodian.

Notices and Change of Address: Any required notice regarding this IRA will be considered effective when we mail it to the last address of the intended recipient which we have in our records. Any notice to be given to us will be considered effective when we actually receive it. You must notify us of any change of address.

Assumptions: We have the right to assume that any information or direction you give us, or any action you take will be proper under this Agreement. We shall not be responsible for your actions or failures to act. Likewise you shall not be responsible for our actions or failures to act.

Service Fees: We have the right to charge an annual service fee or other designated fees (for example, a transfer, rollover or termination fee) for maintaining your IRA. If you do not pay any fee separately, it may be paid from the assets in your IRA. We reserve the right to charge any additional fee upon 30 days notice to you that the fee will be effective.

Self-Directed Investments: We may allow you to direct the investments of your IRA assets in any of the investments which we are authorized to offer for IRAs. We cannot offer any investment advice nor can we exercise any investment discretion regarding the assets in your IRA. In addition, we will not be responsible for any investment decisions you make.

Investment of Amounts in the IRA: We will invest your IRA assets into one or more of the following, as selected by you, which we are authorized to offer, and do in fact offer, as IRA investments:
- Savings Account — Certificate of Deposit — Share Account
- Share Certificate — Any savings instruments which we offer
- Any other investment as directed by you

The investments mentioned above are subject to the by-laws of our institution and all of the Federal and state laws and regulations which apply to us.

Beneficiaries: If you die before you receive all of the amounts in your IRA, payments from your IRA will be made to your beneficiary(ies).

You may designate any person(s) as beneficiary(ies) of your IRA. This designation can only be made on a form prescribed by us, and it will only be effective when it is filed with us during your lifetime. Each Beneficiary designation you file with us will cancel all previous ones. The consent of a Beneficiary shall not be required to revoke a Beneficiary designation. If you do not designate a Beneficiary, your estate will be the Beneficiary.

If you wish, you may specify the method of payment to the Beneficiary(ies). If you don't specify, the Beneficiary(ies) shall have the right to elect the method of payment of his or her distributions. Any specified or elected method of payment must conform with the provisions of Article IV above.

Termination: Either party may terminate this Agreement at any time by giving written notice to the other.

If this Agreement is terminated, we may hold back from your IRA a reasonable amount of money that we believe is necessary to cover any one or more of the following:
- Any expenses or taxes chargeable against your IRA;
- Any penalties associated with the early withdrawal of the savings instrument in your IRA.

If our institution is merged with or bought by another institution, that institution shall become the Custodian of your IRA, but only if it is the type of organization approved by the Internal Revenue Service to hold assets of IRAs.

Changing This Agreement: We can change this Agreement at any time to meet the requirements of the tax laws and regulations.

Withdrawals: All requests for withdrawal shall be in writing on a form provided by or acceptable to us. The reason for the withdrawal and the method of distribution must be stated in writing.

Any withdrawals shall be subject to all applicable tax and other laws and regulations including possible early withdrawal penalties and withholding requirements.

Transfers From Other IRAs: We can receive amounts transferred to this IRA from the Custodian or Trustee of another IRA.

Restrictions On The Fund: Neither you nor any beneficiary may sell, transfer or pledge any interest in your IRA in any manner whatsoever, except as provided by law or this Agreement.

The assets in your IRA shall not be responsible for the debt, contracts or torts of any person entitled to distributions under this Agreement.

What Law Applies: As mentioned above, this Agreement is subject to all applicable Federal and state laws and regulations. If it is necessary to apply any state law to interpret and administer this Agreement, the law of our domicile shall govern.

If any part of this Agreement is held to be illegal or invalid, the remaining parts shall not be affected.

INSTRUCTIONS
Section references are to the Internal Revenue Code

PAPERWORK REDUCTION ACT NOTICE
The Paperwork Reduction Act of 1980 says that we must tell you why we are collecting this information, how it is to be used, and whether you have to provide it. The information is used to determine if you are entitled to a deduction for contributions to this Custodial account. Your completing this information is only required if you want to adopt this model Custodial account.

PURPOSE
This model Custodial account may be used by an individual who wishes to adopt an Individual Retirement Account under Section 408(a). When fully executed by the Depositor and the Custodian not later than the time prescribed by law for filing the Federal income tax return of the Depositor's tax year (including any extensions thereof), a Depositor will have an Individual Retirement Account (IRA) Custodial account which meets the requirements of Section 408(a). This Custodial account must be created in the United States for the exclusive benefit of the Depositor or his/her Beneficiaries.

DEFINITIONS
Custodian: The Custodian must be a bank or savings and loan association as defined in Section 581, a Federally insured credit union, or other person who has the approval of the Internal Revenue Service to act as Custodian.
Depositor: The depositor is the person who establishes the account.

IRA FOR THE NONWORKING SPOUSE
Contributions to an IRA Custodial account for a nonworking spouse must be made to a separate IRA Custodial account established by the nonworking spouse.

This form may be used to establish the IRA Custodial account for the nonworking spouse.

An employee's social security number will serve as the identification number of his or her Individual Retirement Account. An employer identification number is not required for each Individual Retirement Account, nor for a common fund created for Individual Retirement Accounts.

For more information, get a copy of the required disclosure statement from your Custodian or get Publication 590, *Tax Information on Individual Retirement Arrangements,* from your local Internal Revenue Service Office.

SPECIFIC INSTRUCTIONS
Article IV: Distributions made under this Article may be made in a single sum, periodic payment, or a combination of both. The distribution option should be reviewed in the year the Depositor reaches age 70½ to make sure the requirements of Section 408(a)(6) have been met. For example, if a Depositor elects distributions over a period permitted in (d) or (e) of Article IV, the period may not extend beyond the life expectancy of the Depositor at age 70½ (under option [d]), or the joint life and last survivor expectancy of the Depositor (at age 70½) and the Depositor's spouse [under option (e)]. For this purpose, life expectancies must be determined by using the expected return multiples in Section 1.72-9 of the Income Tax Regulations (26CFR Part 1). The balance in the account, as of the beginning of each tax year beginning on or after the Depositor reaches age 70½, will be used in computing the payments described in (d) and (e) of Article IV. Article IV does not preclude a mode of distribution different from those described in (a) through (e) of Article IV prior to the close of the tax year of the Depositor in which he/she reaches age 70½.

Article IX: This Article and any that follow it may incorporate additional provisions that are agreed upon by the Depositor and Custodian to complete the Agreement. These may include, for example, definitions, investment powers, voting rights, exculpatory provisions, amendments and terminations, removal of Custodian, Custodian's fees, state law requirements, beginning date of distributions, accepting only cash, treatment of excess contributions, prohibited transactions with the Depositors, etc. Use additional pages if necessary and attach them to this form.

Note: This form may be reproduced and reduced in size for adoption to passbook card purposes.

ACCOUNTHOLDER COPY
#98 (8/85)

©1985 Universal Pensions, Inc., Brainerd, MN 56401

Disclosure Statement

As IRA trustees, financial institutions are required by law to furnish a disclosure statement to every customer who establishes an IRA. The *disclosure statement* is a nontechnical explanation of all of the IRA rules, terms and conditions that affect the account holder. For every disclosure not made, or improperly made, the IRS can charge the institution a penalty fine. A sample of a disclosure form is shown in Figure 4-3.

Disclosures need to be made only once for each IRA. Financial institutions have two options regarding the timing of disclosures under IRA law. First, the disclosure statement may be furnished seven days *before* the date on which the account is to be opened. Or, second, disclosure may be made *on* the date of the account opening. In this case, it must be stated in the trust account agreement that the participant has seven business days *after* the opening of the IRA to revoke the agreement. The institution can require that the revocation be oral or written, or both.

If a material adverse change in the disclosure statement, or a change in the trust account agreement, occurs during the seven-day revocation period, amendments must be furnished to the participant, who then has an *additional* seven-day right of revocation.[3] This new revocation period begins when the participant receives the material, which is deemed to occur seven days after the institution mails the changes. In effect, the IRA law effectively permits participants a 14-day revocation period following the mailing of amendments.

Should a financial institution subsequently amend its IRA terms and conditions, disclosure must be made to all participants within 30 days after either the effective date or the adoption of the amendments, whichever occurs later. The institution does not have to repeat information in the first disclosure statement that remains unchanged. However, if any terms or conditions in the first disclosure statement are affected by the subsequent amendments, this information must be included in the new disclosure.

When opening new IRAs, institutions should temporarily supplement their IRA disclosure statements with copies of the latest issue of IRS Publication 590. This publication provides a general explanation of IRA changes made by the 1984 and 1986 tax acts. Until the IRS issues revised IRA forms, the latest Publication 590 will satisfy the IRS disclosure updating requirements.

For existing IRAs, institutions are not required to provide amendments and new disclosures to their IRA customers until the IRS issues its IRA revisions. Many institutions voluntarily provide their customers with periodic IRA information updates.

The disclosure statement usually has two main sections. One section covers statutory and regulatory requirements about the operation and tax treatment of IRAs. The second section covers financial disclosures.

Regulatory disclosure. The following items offer examples of the data contained in the regulatory disclosure section. These items provide the participant with both general information about how IRAs work and specific information about a sponsor's IRA. The information provided in this first section typically includes the following:
- circumstances and procedures for revocation,

FIGURE 4-3
Sample Disclosure Statement

INDIVIDUAL RETIREMENT ACCOUNT DISCLOSURE STATEMENT

NOTE: Because of the possible personal implications of the individual retirement account tax rules, any individual having questions regarding applicability of the information in this disclosure statement to his own situation and actions should consult his own tax advisor.

I. **LEGAL REQUIREMENTS FOR THE OPERATION AND TAX TREATMENT OF INDIVIDUAL RETIREMENT ACCOUNTS; 7-DAY REVOCATION PROCEDURE**

   A. **INTRODUCTION.** This disclosure statement describes the official government rules regarding the operation and tax treatment of your Individual Retirement Account ("IRA"). Copies of the trust agreement establishing the IRA and the rules for the class of savings deposits in which the IRA funds are invested accompany this disclosure statement.

   B. **7-DAY REVOCATION PROCEDURE.** Regulations of the IRS provide that a disclosure statement may be given to the participant on the date the IRA is established if the participant is able to revoke the IRA within 7 days after that date. Otherwise, the disclosure statement must be provided to the participant at least 7 days before the IRA is established.
   Since your IRA described in this statement provides for delivery of this disclosure statement to you on the date you establish your IRA, you are entitled to revoke the IRA within seven days after such date. You may revoke only by written notice mailed or delivered to: Attention: IRA Revocation Administrator in care of the Trustee at the address listed on the Application.

   If mailed, the revocation notice shall be deemed mailed on the date of the postmark (or if by registered or certified mail, the date of registration or certification) if deposited in the mail in the United States in an envelope or other appropriate wrapper, first class postage prepaid, properly addressed to the person designated above by name or title. Upon revocation within the seven day period, you will be entitled to a return of the entire amount paid by you into the IRA without adjustment for penalties or other charges.

   C. **THE IRA.** An IRA is a trust account which allows you, if you are eligible, to accumulate funds for retirement under favorable tax conditions. If the IRA satisfies Internal Revenue Code requirements, your contributions to it generally are deductible from your gross income and the IRA (including earnings) is not taxed until distribution occurs or the arrangement ceases to be an IRA because you or your beneficiary has engaged in a prohibited transaction as described in Part II below.

   D. **ELIGIBILITY.** If you have compensation which is includible in gross income and you do not attain age 70½ during the taxable year, you may contribute to an IRA under this agreement. Eligible "compensation" includes salaries, wages, professional fees, self-employment income (less amounts contributed to a Keogh plan) and other income for personal services which is includible in your gross income. Income from property, such as dividends, interest or rent, and pension or annuity payments or other deferred compensation do not qualify as "compensation" for IRA purposes.

   E. **QUALIFICATION OF AN IRA.** The Form 5305 agreement under which your IRA is established has been approved as to form by the Internal Revenue Service. (IRS approval is a determination only as to form and not as to the merits of the IRA.) When you fully execute an application adopting this agreement and the IRA is administered in accordance with the following rules, you will have an IRA which meets the requirements of Internal Revenue Code Section 408(a). The trust must be created in the United States for the exclusive use of you or your beneficiaries.

   1. Limitation on Contributions. Deductible contributions must be made in cash and, except for an employer's simplified employee pension plan (SEP) contributions, cannot exceed the lesser of $2,000 or the amount of your compensation for any taxable year. If both you and your spouse receive compensation as defined in the preceding paragraph during the year and are otherwise eligible, each of you may contribute to his or her own IRA. The contribution limitations are applicable to the separate compensation of each of you without regard to any state community property laws.

   2. Limitation on Investment of Trust Funds. No part of the IRA trust funds may be invested in life insurance contracts or in collectibles as defined in Internal Revenue Code Section 408(m).

   3. Investment and Holding of Contributions. Contributions under the IRA are held in a trust account for the exclusive benefit of you, your surviving spouse or any other beneficiary you name. Your beneficiary may be your estate, a dependent or any other person you designate in writing delivered to the trustee. Your interest in the IRA is non-forfeitable. The trustee maintains a separate account or record of your IRA which is available for inspection during the trustee's regular business hours. The funds in this trust will be invested in savings deposits chosen by you from among the classes of deposits offered for the investment of IRA funds. The trustee has discretion to determine what types of deposits will be included in such classes. However, if permitted by law and by the terms of the IRA trust agreement, the trustee may invest part or all of the funds in other investments as directed by you. You are solely responsible for directing investment of the funds accumulated in the IRA trust in savings deposits or other authorized investments, and the trustee will carry out its responsibilities in this regard only in response to your specific written instructions.

   4. Distribution of Funds: (a) To You. Distribution of benefits without IRS penalty tax for premature distribution may begin as soon as you attain age 59½ or become disabled but must begin before the close of the taxable year in which you attain age 70½. Article

IV, paragraph 1 of the IRA trust agreement sets forth a number of optional methods for distributing the funds in the IRA. You may elect any of these methods of distribution. A "minimum distribution" is required to be made to you each year beginning with the year in which you attain age 70½, such distribution to be determined by dividing the entire balance at the beginning of each year by your life expectancy (or joint life and last survivor expectancy of you and your spouse, if applicable) determined as of the date you attain age 70½, reduced by the number of years elapsed since you attained age 70½. See Part II paragraph D of this statement for a description of the penalty tax which may be incurred if a distribution is "insufficient," that is, less than the minimum required to be distributed during any taxable year when you are age 70½ or older. If you fail to elect a method of distribution before the end of the taxable year in which you attain age 70½, distribution of the full balance in the IRA must be made to you in a single sum prior to the close of that taxable year.

(b) In the Event of Your Death. (1) If you (or your surviving spouse) die before the entire IRA balance has been distributed, the law requires that the balance in the account be distributed to the beneficiary within five years after your death (or the death of your surviving spouse). Distribution within 5 years is not required: if distributions over a period certain commenced before your death; the period certain is not in excess of your life expectancy or the joint life and last survivor life expectancy of you and your spouse; and distributions to your beneficiary continue over that period.

(2) In the case of an "inherited" IRA, that is, when a person other than your spouse acquires your IRA because of your death, that person is prohibited from making deductible contributions to such IRA and also is prohibited from continuing the tax deferral afforded by rolling over or transferring the funds from such IRA to another IRA or from another IRA into such IRA.

F. **DEDUCTIBLE CONTRIBUTIONS.** Deductions from gross income for IRA contributions are subject to the following limits:

1. "Regular" IRA. Your contributions to an IRA except for rollovers are deductible up to the lesser of $2,000 or the amount of compensation includible in your gross income for the taxable year. No deduction is allowed for contributions made during or after the taxable year in which you attain age 70½. (For rules relating to deduction limits on SEP contributions, see paragraph 4 below.) The IRA deduction is an adjustment to gross income which may be taken whether or not you itemize deductions on your tax return. No deduction is allowed for any contribution in excess of the maximum deductible amount. You may make contributions for a given taxable year during such year or at any time prior to your tax return filing date for such year (including extensions).

2. Spousal IRA Contributions. You may make and deduct a contribution to your spouse's IRA in a taxable year if: (a) you and your spouse file a joint return; (b) your spouse receives no compensation in taxable year; (c) your spouse is under age 70½; (d) the aggregate amount of the contributions to your spouse's IRA and your own does not exceed the lesser of $2,250 or the amount of your compensation for such year. The contribution to either spouse's IRA may not exceed $2,000. Although you may not contribute to your own IRA if you have reached age 70½, you may contribute to your spouse's IRA if your spouse is under age 70½.

3. Employer or Employee Association Contributions. Under section 408(c) of the Internal Revenue Code, to the extent that an employee association or an employer pays any amount to an IRA account on behalf of an individual, such payment constitutes taxable income to the individual. This amount, however, is deductible from gross income as an amount paid to the IRA on behalf of the individual provided that it does not exceed the limitations on deductions described in paragraphs (1) and (2). If the employer or employee association contributes less than the maximum permitted, the employee may contribute the difference but the aggregate may not exceed the regular or spousal limits.

4. SEP Contributions. If your employer makes contributions to your IRA under a SEP plan, such contributions are includible in your gross income and deductible by you (even if you are age 70½ or older). Your employer who establishes a SEP plan will provide you with information about eligibility, contributions, deductibility and related matters. You are permitted to deduct both the employer's SEP contributions and any contributions you make to your own or your spouse's IRA subject to the limitations described in Internal Revenue Code Section 219 and this Section F.

5. Divorced Spouse Contributions. A divorced spouse may make IRA contributions based on alimony received from the former spouse if the divorced spouse's IRA has been in existence for five years preceding the year the divorce occurred, the former spouse has made spousal contributions to that IRA for three out of the five years, and the contribution does not exceed the lesser of $1,125 or the amount of compensation and alimony which is includible in the divorced spouse's gross income. Without regard to the receipt of alimony, if the divorced spouse has compensation exceeding $1,125, a regular IRA contribution may be made up to the lesser of $2,000 or total compensation.

G. **INCOME TAX TREATMENT OF WITHDRAWALS AND DISTRIBUTIONS.** Funds generally cannot be distributed from your IRA before you attain age 59½ without certain adverse tax consequences. Distributions prior to reaching age 59½ (including amounts deemed distributed as a result of prohibited transactions or use of part or all of the IRA as security for a loan) are considered to be premature distributions. In addition to being fully taxable to you as ordinary income at the time of distribution, such premature distributions are subject to an IRS penalty tax of 10 percent. The premature distribution restrictions do not apply to distributions made on account of your death or certified disability or under certain conditions, your divorce.

Distributions occurring after you reach age 59½, die or are disabled are not subject to IRS penalty tax but are taxable at ordinary income tax rates. A distribution from an IRA is not entitled to the special income tax treatment - such as 10 year averaging - which may be accorded lump sum payments by section 402(a)(2) and (e) of the Code. However, the 5-year income averaging provisions of sections 1301 to 1304 of the Code may apply. Income tax will be withheld from your IRA distributions unless you make a written election otherwise.

H. **ROLLOVER CONTRIBUTIONS.** If you receive a lump sum distribution or a plan termination distribution within one taxable year from a qualified employee benefit plan (including a Keogh plan), you may "roll over" into an IRA all or any part of the distribution within 60 days of the date you receive it. No tax deduction is allowed for the amount of a rollover contribution to an IRA, but your tax deferral

FIGURE 4-3, continued

for such amount continues until it is subsequently distributed.

A rollover of part or all of a lump sum or plan termination distribution may be made by your surviving spouse who receives such distribution from your employee benefit plan after your death. Your spouse may roll such a distribution over only into an IRA.

In the case of rollovers from qualified plans, the amount rolled over must consist solely of employer and deductible voluntary employee contributions, and interest earned on these or on other employee contributions. Any part of the distribution you retain, except your own tax-paid (nondeductible) contributions, is subject to income tax, while amounts properly rolled over are not taxed until distributed from the rollover account. If otherwise eligible to do so, you make deductible IRA contributions to a rollover IRA established with a qualified plan on Code Section 403(b) annuity distribution, but if this occurs, the law may preclude further rollover of the funds back into a qualified plan or Code Section 403(b) annuity.

You may convert non-cash property distributed from a qualified plan into cash by means of a **bona fide** (arms-length) sale and roll over part or all of the proceeds into an IRA or another qualified plan within the usual 60-day period after the distribution.

You may withdraw all or part of the balance in your IRA and roll over all or a part of the amount withdrawn into another IRA without adverse tax consequences. There can only be one such tax-free rollover from a given IRA to another IRA within a one-year period. This limitation does not apply to rollovers of funds between qualified employer plans and IRAs, or to direct transfers between IRA trustees.

I. **TAXPAYER REPORTING REQUIREMENTS.** If a transaction has occurred for which a penalty tax is imposed, such as an excess contribution, a premature distribution or an excess accumulation (insufficient distribution), you are required by the Internal Revenue Service to attach to your annual income tax return an information return Form 5329 prescribed for reporting such transaction and calculating the penalty tax due.

II. **ADDITIONAL PROVISIONS AND PROHIBITIONS**

A. **PROHIBITED TRANSACTIONS.** You, your spouse and your beneficiaries are prohibited from engaging in any prohibited transactions (within the meaning of Internal Revenue Code section 4975) with respect to your IRA. If such transactions occur, the IRA will cease to be qualified and will lose its exemption from tax. The full IRA balance will be treated as having been distributed for purposes of income taxes and penalty taxes. The trustee and other disqualified parties also are prohibited from engaging in any prohibited transaction with respect to the IRA and will be subject to penalties unless a statutory or administrative exemption has been granted.

B. **USE OF IRA ASSETS AS SECURITY FOR LOANS.** If you borrow money and use all or any portion of your IRA as security, the portion of the IRA so used will be deemed to be distributed to you. In this event, if you have not attained age 59½ and are not disabled, the distribution not only will be fully taxable at ordinary income tax rates but also will be subject to the 10 percent penalty tax discussed above for premature distributions. Consequently, pledging the IRA assets as security for a loan is specifically prohibited.

C. **PENALTY FOR EXCESS CONTRIBUTIONS.** An "excess contribution" is a contribution to an IRA in a taxable year in excess of the maximum amount deductible or permitted to be rolled over into an IRA for that taxable year. A penalty tax equal to 6 percent of the amount of the excess contribution is imposed on you if you have an excess contribution in your IRA as of the close of any taxable year. The penalty may be avoided if you withdraw the excess contribution from the IRA before the date for filing your federal tax return for the year in which the excess contribution was made, and if you do not claim a deduction for it. Such timely withdrawal will avoid the 6 percent penalty even if contribution limitations are exceeded. The earnings attributable to the excess contribution also must be withdrawn and included in your gross income for the year in which the excess contribution was made.

Withdrawal of an excess contribution after the tax return filing date will not avoid imposition of the 6 percent penalty, but will avoid that penalty in future years following the withdrawal. When such a delayed withdrawal of an excess contribution is made, if you have not reached age 59½ and are not disabled, and if either the aggregate contributions for the taxable year in which the excess contribution was made exceeded $2,250 or a deduction was claimed for the amount withdrawn, that amount will be includible in taxable income and will be subject to a premature distribution penalty tax of 10 percent. If an excess contribution is attributable to a rollover made because of erroneous tax information supplied by an employer upon which an individual reasonably relied, such excess may be removed, even though the $2,250 limit is exceeded, without incurring the 10 percent penalty.

If not withdrawn, and if no deduction has been claimed, the excess contribution may be corrected by applying it against your deductible limit in a following year. For example, if you had compensation of only $1,700 but contributed $2,000 for an IRA in year one, and did not withdraw the $300 excess contribution by the due date for filing your federal income tax return, you could only claim a $1,700 tax deduction and you would be charged an $18.00 penalty ($300 x .06) with respect to year one. In year two (assuming you then are entitled to make a $2,000 contribution), you may eliminate the $300 excess contribution by making a contribution of only $1,700 to the IRA while claiming $2,000 as a tax deduction for year two. The $300 excess contribution then ceases to be an excess contribution, and the penalty would be eliminated for year two. If an excess contribution is not "cured", either by undercontributing or by removal, the 6 percent penalty continues to apply to each year in which there is an excess contribution remaining in the IRA.

D. **PENALTY FOR CERTAIN ACCUMULATIONS.** After you reach age 70½, or if you die and payments are to be made to your beneficiary, if the required "minimum distributions" described in Part I(E)(4)(a) or (b) do not occur within the time required by law, a penalty tax may be applied equal to 50 percent of the difference between the amount required to be distributed and the amount actually distributed each year. The Secretary of the Treasury may waive the penalty if the inadequate distribution is due to reasonable error and reasonable steps are being taken to correct the situation.

E. **ESTATE AND GIFT TAXES.** Code Section 2039(e), which provides a $100,000 exemption from estate tax for annuities and certain other arrangements under IRA trusts and plans, and Code Section 2517, which relates to exemption from gift tax of certain annuities under qualified plans, apply to yor IRA. Under Code Section 2039(e), your IRA funds are excludible from your estate if distributable to your beneficiary (other than the executor of your estate in such capacity) in the form of an annuity contract or other arrangement providing for a series of substantially equal periodic payments for life or over a period extending for at least 36 months after the date of your death. Section 2517 provides that exercise or nonexercise of an option under your IRA whereby amounts will become payable to a beneficiary will not be considered a transfer for gift tax purposes.

F. **ADDITIONAL INFORMATION.** Additional information regarding the rules governing your IRA is provided in IRS Publication 590, which may be obtained from any district office of the Internal Revenue Service.

III. FINANCIAL DISCLOSURE

A. VALUE OF YOUR IRA. The balance in your IRA can be expected to increase as a direct result of your contributions and the return on the investment of accumulated contributions and accumulated earnings. **Either paragraph 1 or paragraph 2 below, depending upon the nature of the investments made, will provide information to you regarding the projected financial future of your IRA.**

(1) This paragraph (1) provides a financial projection of the growth in value of your IRA, on the assumption that the balance in your IRA will be invested in one or more of the deposits included in the class or classes of deposits designated by the institution for the investment of IRA funds.

When funds are invested in certain types of deposits, it is possible to make a reasonable projection as to the amount of money that will be available at specified times in the future if certain assumptions are made. If other investments are to be made pursuant to the IRA trust agreement, the financial disclosure information provided in paragraph (2) below will apply.

The assumptions are that annual contributions are made in the amount of $1,000 on the first day of each taxable year, and that the funds are invested in a _____ at an interest rate of _____ percent, compounded
(type of deposit)

_____, for a term of _____. If the funds are invested in fixed-term
(interval)   (number of days, months or years)
certificates of deposit, the projected amounts may be reduced by application of a certificate penalty for withdrawal prior to maturity as required by federal regulation under certain circumstances. The projected total amounts accumulated in the IRA are shown in the first column; the second column below reflects the projected amounts available after imposition of such a penalty.

Under the stated assumptions, the projected account balances would be as follows:

	Total accumulation	Amount available to you after premature withdrawal, if any
At end of first year............	$ _____	$ _____
At end of second year.........	$ _____	$ _____
At end of third year...........	$ _____	$ _____
At end of fourth year..........	$ _____	$ _____
At end of fifth year............	$ _____	$ _____

These amounts, as well as the amounts below, are projections only. The rate of interest payable on the savings deposits in which the funds are invested may be subject to change as may be provided by the deposit contract, and cannot be guaranteed at a constant rate for the duration of the IRA. Furthermore, if IRA funds are withdrawn at the periods described above, and you have not attained age 59½ or become disabled, the distribution, if not rolled over into another IRA, also will be subject to the 10 percent penalty tax imposed by IRS upon premature distribution.

Since the purpose of the individual retirement plan is to provide you with income in your retirement years, the most important feature of an account plan is the benefits the IRA will provide at retirement age. Assuming the same level of contributions, the same rate of interest on the savings account as stated above and absence of prior distributions from the IRA, the projected amount available to you would be as follows:

At End of Year in   60 years of age................................... $ _____
Which You Attain: 65 years of age................................... $ _____
                      70 years of age................................... $ _____

These projections at the specified ages reflect an assumption that the penalty for early withdrawal from a fixed-term certificate _____ be waived.
                    (will or will not)

However, you are not required to withdraw the entire balance upon attaining a retirement age, but may elect a later time (but not later than the last day of the year in which you reach age 70½) and any of the optional methods for distribution set forth in the IRA agreement. Each option will have an actuarial value at the date distribution is commenced equal to the amount that could have been withdrawn from the account in a single sum if none of the elections had been made.

(2) This paragraph (2) provides you with information as to how the net amount available to you is determined in the event that an actual financial projection cannot reasonably be made:

(a) Type of charge and amount thereof which may be made against a contribution: _____
_____

(b) Method used for computing and allocating annual earnings: _____
_____

(c) Charge or charges that may be applied to such earnings in determining the net amount of money available to you: _____
_____

Method used in computing such charges: _____
_____

(d) Growth in the value of your account is neither guaranteed nor projected.
(e) The following is the portion of every $1,000 contributed that is attributable to the cost of life insurance for each year during which contributions are to be made: _____. Any amount shown here is not deductible.

B. ROLLOVER PROJECTION. If the initial and only contribution to the IRA is a rollover, the projection in III(A)(1) above is based on the assumption that such rollover is made in the amount of $1,000 on the first day of the first year and that no other contributions are to be made.

C. TRUSTEE'S CHARGES. The trustee may impose a reasonable charge for administering the trust, preparing reports, keeping records and such other services as may be required to administer the trust. The trustee may also charge the trust account the reasonable costs of fiduciary insurance, counsel fees and reasonable compensation for its services as a trustee. Such fees, if any will be charged directly to and deducted from the trust account, unless you pay them out-of-pocket.
Current fees or fee schedule:
_____
_____

SAF Systems and Forms 11562 (7/84)   © 1984 United States League of Savings Institutions
U.S.L. IRA Trust Plan

including the name, title, address and telephone number of the institution employee designated to receive notification of revocation;
- the IRA's tax status;
- whether or not the IRA is approved by the Internal Revenue Service;
- contribution provisions and rules, including rules on treatments of excess contributions and assessed penalties;
- distribution rules, including calculation of minimum distribution and penalties for underdistributions made after age 70½;
- estate and gift tax exemptions;
- rollover provisions to and from IRAs;
- the participant's reporting requirements; and
- information on spousal IRAs.

Financial disclosure. The financial institution is required to project the growth of the account in a number of ways:
- The calculation is based on an assumed level: that an annual contribution of $1,000 will be made on the *first day* of each calendar year, regardless of the actual contribution being made.
- When an IRA is established with a rollover or transfer, the financial projection is based on the assumption that the account holder will make a one-time, $1,000 deposit.
- The interest rate used in the projection is to be no greater than, and terms no different from, those currently in effect. In other words, the IRA rates and method of compounding that are given in the institution's statement of terms and conditions are used as the basis of this calculation.
- The account value must be shown during its first five years, taking into consideration any penalties assessed by the financial institution for early withdrawal of certificates or redemption fees.
- The account value at the end of the years in

which the account holder will attain the ages of 60, 65 and 70 must be shown. The account holder's actual age should be used when projecting these future values.
- The projected account values must also reflect any annual service or trustee fees, transfer, rollover or transaction fees.

If an institution can guarantee—or can reasonably project—the growth of an IRA, the institution is required to make this disclosure. For self-directed IRAs, however, the required financial disclosures are different because a self-directed IRA program allows for investments to be made outside of the financial institution trustee. Because of the uncertainty of growth of such outside investments, the institution cannot give reasonable projections of future values. Therefore, the IRS requires the following financial disclosure information to be provided for self-directed IRAs:
- the investments to be offered through the self-directed program;
- the fees that may be charged in a self-directed IRA; and
- how earnings are computed on available investments.

Also for self-directed IRAs, any other information that would aid the account holder should be provided, such as the following:
- any relationship between the financial institution and an affiliated brokerage firm; or
- the procedure an account holder must follow to request an investment transaction.

All of the above regulatory and financial disclosures are specifically required by U.S. Treasury regulations and, therefore, must be complied with.[4] Because financial institutions have been fined for not providing proper disclosures, finan-

136   IRA Basics

FIGURE 4-4
Designation of Beneficiary

INDIVIDUAL RETIREMENT ACCOUNT (TRUST) APPLICATION AND BENEFICIARY DESIGNATION

File or Account Number _____

State of _____ }
County of _____ } SS

TRUSTEE NAME
Street Address
City, State, Zip Code

Name of Grantor: _____
Social Security No.: _____ Date of Birth: _____
Grantor's Address: _____ Home Phone: _____
City: _____ State _____ Zip Code: _____

Amount of Initial Deposit $ _____ : Allocated: $_____ for tax year _____
                                                       $_____ for tax year _____

If not regular IRA Contribution, Indicate type: ___Rollover ___Spousal ___SEP ___Transfer ___Divorced Sp. ___Other

Subject to the conditions below, I hereby designate the following as my beneficiary(ies) under the United States League Form 5305 IRA Trust Agreement ("the Agreement") hereby revoking all prior designations, if any, made by me:

NAME/RELATIONSHIP   MAILING ADDRESS

Primary
Beneficiary(ies): _____   _____
                  _____   _____

Contingent
Beneficiary(ies): _____   _____
                  _____   _____

Conditions of Beneficiary Designation:
1. This designation is subject to all the terms and provisions of the Agreement and shall be effective only if received by the Trustee prior to the death of the person executing it.
2. This designation applies to the participant's entire interest, if any, in the trust assets remaining undistributed at the participant's or beneficiary's death, as the case may be; provided, however, that the designation shall not apply if the assets are used to purchase an annuity contract, it being intended that the payment of benefits in that event shall be governed by the settlement options and beneficiary designations provided for under such contract.
3. Unless otherwise provided on the face of this designation, each payment to be made pursuant to this designation: (a) shall be paid in equal shares to primary beneficiaries who are living at the time such payment becomes due or (b) if no primary beneficiary is living at the time, such payment shall be made in equal shares to the contingent beneficiaries who are then living.
4. This designation may be changed only by the filing of a written change of beneficiary designation with the Trustee.

By my signature below, I apply, and Trustee by its signature accepts my application, to participate in the Individual Retirement Trust Account Program of the Trustee subject to the terms of the Agreement and the rules of the financial institution applicable to the savings deposit or class of deposits offered to participants in such program for the investment of contributions thereunder.

I acknowledge that I have received a copy of the rules of deposit classification and an IRA disclosure statement. The Trustee is authorized to act without further inquiry in accordance with writings bearing my signature. I understand that I may revoke the Agreement by written notice to the Trustee within seven (7) days after the date of the Agreement as specified below.

Witness (Required for Beneficiary Designation):   Date: _____

_____
(Witness should not be a beneficiary)   _____
Address of Witness: _____   (Signature of Grantor)

_____ _____ _____   _____
(City)   (State)   (Zip Code)   (Name of Financial Institution)

                                                          as Trustee under the Agreement hereby acknowledges receipt of the above Designation of Beneficiary and Grantor's Application to participate in the Individual Retirement Trust Account Program.

                                                          By: _____
                                                                      (Authorized Officer)

SAF Systems and Forms 11511 (3-85)   **SAF Systems and Forms**
                                                          © 1984 United States League of Savings Institutions

cial institution employees should make sure each customer receives a correctly completed disclosure.

Designation of Beneficiary
An IRA participant may designate a beneficiary as recipient of any assets remaining in the IRA at the participant's death. Both primary and contingent beneficiaries may be named, and the IRA participant may change the beneficiaries at any time by completing another form. For example, Al Mader, an IRA participant, may name his wife, Yvette, as primary beneficiary. Al also may name his children, Stephanie and Matthew, as contingent beneficiaries. In the event that Yvette dies before Al, Al's children would inherit his IRA. Typically beneficiaries are family relations, although an IRA participant may designate any person or entity, for example, a friend, corporation or charity, as beneficiary. If no beneficiary is designated, the participant's estate will inherit the funds from the IRA account.

The designation of beneficiary as shown in Figure 4-4 contains the IRA account number, the grantor's date of birth, and the signature and address of the witness. The witness should not be a beneficiary, but may be a friend of the participant or an institution employee. An officer or other authorized employee of the institution also signs the form to acknowledge its receipt. A copy is then given to the participant, and the original is kept in the participant's file at the institution.

Deposit Information
Whenever an IRA is established or a subsequent deposit is made, the institution should obtain and document the information that is necessary to complete required reporting.

This information is:
- the deposit amount;
- the type of IRA deposit being made—for example, regular, spousal, SEP, direct transfer or rollover;
- the tax year for which the deposit is being made;
- any necessary investment information that pertains to the specific transaction; and
- the account holder's signature.

Some institutions have developed special deposit slips that the participant uses to make an IRA deposit. A sample IRA deposit slip is shown in Figure 4-5.

Optional Documentation

In addition to executing the four documents required to establish an IRA—the plan agreement, disclosure statement, designation of beneficiary

FIGURE 4-5
IRA Deposit Slip

IRA DEPOSIT AUTHORIZATION		
DATE _____ SOCIAL SECURITY NUMBER_____ ACCOUNT NO. _____		
NAME _____		
ADDRESS _____		

Type of Deposit:	Deposit Allocated	CASH		
☐ Regular or Spousal	$_____ for tax year _____	CHECKS		
☐ Transfer	$_____ for tax year _____			
☐ Rollover				
☐ Other _____		TOTAL		
Under penalties of perjury, I certify that my contribution relates to the tax year I have indicated.		LESS CASH RECEIVED		
Depositor Signature _____		NET DEPOSIT		

and deposit information—individual institutions may require their employees to complete additional documentation. IRA counselors also may prepare a certificate of deposit, a deposit account passbook, or some other evidence of the IRA deposit such as a statement or receipt. At institutions using computerized record-keeping systems, the IRA counselor may complete an input document with all of the information necessary to enter the new account on the computer's records. Many institutions use signature cards to document ownership of their IRAs. Also, some institutions use an IRA worksheet to shorten the time it takes for their customers to open IRAs. Descriptions of these two optional documents follow.

Signature card. A signature card is a common way for institutions to show that an account relationship exists. However, more advanced methods, such as microfilm or electronic means of identification, may be used instead of a signature card.

At one time signature cards were required. Since April 9, 1986, however, FSLIC-insured institutions no longer are required to maintain signature cards for trust accounts such as IRAs, qualified plans, and revocable and irrevocable trusts. However, account records still must maintain proof that a trust relationship exists. This proof is needed in case of an insurance claim.[5] Therefore, regulations still require FSLIC-insured institutions to maintain proof that a trust account relationship exists, but no longer require the use of a signature card as the only way to show this proof. Even so, many institutions continue to use signature cards because a signature card is still the easiest way for them to prove that the trust account relationship exists. Also, depending on an institution's administrative procedures, signature cards may be the most convenient way of identifying customers.

The signature card as shown in Figure 4-6 contains the following information: the participant's Social Security number; the IRA account number; the institution's name, as trustee; the date the trust account agreement was executed; and the participant's name, as grantor. Both the participant and an officer or other authorized employee of the institution sign the card, indicating their acceptance of the terms of the account. The signature card is retained in the participant's file.

IRA worksheet. The IRA worksheet shown in Figure 4-7 provides a way to organize the IRA participant's identifying information. When such a form is used, it is generally the first one the counselor completes because it contains all or most of the information necessary to complete the other IRA documents. The worksheet often shows, in addition to the participant's name and address, the designated beneficiaries and their relationship to the participant, the type of IRA plan chosen and the amount of the initial contribution. In some cases, additional information may be gathered for marketing purposes. Since this form is used chiefly to facilitate the preparation of other IRA documents, a copy is not generally furnished to the participant.

The format of and the information on the worksheet can vary depending on the needs of the institution. For example, a worksheet designed to increase efficiency when opening accounts would be helpful if many customers are waiting, if a customer is in a hurry or if someone wishes to open an IRA through the mail. In these situations,

FIGURE 4-6
IRA Signature Card

(Grantor's Soc. Sec. No.)

Acct. No. ______________

______ Suburban Federal Savings and Loan Association ______, Trustee
(Name of Savings Institution)

The undersigned, as Trustee, officially affirmed on ______________
(Date)
by a trust agreement known as the United States League of Savings Institutions Form 5305 Individual Retirement Trust Account as executed by
____
(Grantor)
hereby applies for a savings account in the savings institution specified as trustee above and for the issuance of evidence thereof. In consideration of your acceptance of this application, the undersigned hereby certifies that the funds which are offered to you concurrently herewith for placement in a savings account and any funds which later may be placed in the same savings account are funds properly within its custody which may be lawfully invested in or placed in the same savings account in said institution in accordance with authority duly vested in the undersigned as fiduciary, all as described above. A specimen signature of the Trustee is shown below and you are hereby authorized to act without further inquiry in accordance with writings bearing such signature, or the signature of any duly authorized agent of the Trustee. You are authorized to supply any endorsement for the undersigned on any check or other instrument tendered for this account and you are hereby relieved of any liability in connection with collection of such items which are handled by you without negligence, and you shall not be liable for the acts of your agents, sub-agents or others or for any casualty. Withdrawals may not be made on account of such items until collected, and any amount not collected may be charged back to this account, including expense incurred, and any other outside expense incurred relative to this account may be charged to it. In this instrument except as otherwise indicated the singular includes the plural.

For identification:

Account of: ______________
(Grantor)

Suburban Federal Savings and Loan Association
(Name of Trustee Savings Institution)

____
(Signature of Grantor)

By ______________
(Agent)

11504 Fiduciary Savings Account (I.R.A.) 2/84

SAF Systems and Forms

institution employees can have the customer fill out the worksheet; then the employee prepares the required IRA documents from the worksheet information and mails the documents to the customer to sign and return. Although the use of IRA worksheets is not a legal requirement, many institutions consider them valuable administrative aids.

Conduct Follow-Up Programs

After opening an IRA with a knowledgeable, friendly IRA counselor, a new participant is likely

FIGURE 4-7
IRA Worksheet

IRA WORKSHEET

Participant Information

Indicate Type of Account Desired
☐ IRA ☐ IRA-SEP ☐ IRA Rollover (Establish Eligibility) ☐ IRA-Spousal

Participant	**Spouse**
Full Name	Name
Social Security No.	Social Security No.
Birth Date	Birth Date
Place of Birth	**Telephone**
Mother's Full Maiden Name	Business ( )
	Home ( )
	Other ( )

Mailing Address and Zip Code

Primary Beneficiary

Complete Name/Relationship

Telephone: Business	Home
( )	( )

Primary Beneficiary(ies) Mailing Address and Zip Code

IRA Worksheet Continued

IRA WORKSHEET, Continued

Contingent Beneficiary(ies)

Complete Name

Relationship

Mailing Address

Telephone
Business ( )
Home ( )

Complete Name

Relationship

Mailing Address

Telephone
Business ( )
Home ( )

☐ Additional Contingent Beneficiary(ies) Listed on Back

Contribution

Initial Contribution
$

Source of Funds
New $

Date

Spousal Contribution
$

Home $

to be appreciative and, as a result, responsive to follow-up programs. Many financial institutions make use of follow-up programs, such as a letter of thanks, to formally acknowledge the institution's appreciation for new participants' business. Follow-up programs provide an additional opportunity for institutions to make IRA participants "part of the family." Following this reasoning, some institutions integrate follow-up programs with promotional materials. The promotional materials invite the new customers to take full advantage of the broad range of services offered by the institution in the future. Market research can be used effectively to identify which particular services ought to be emphasized in any specially designated promotional literature enclosed for cross-selling purposes.

Servicing and Maintaining IRAs

Once an IRA is opened, a new set of activities begins. It is very important for existing IRA accounts to be administered accurately and in a legally correct manner. Necessary administrative procedures for existing IRAs can be grouped into the following five major activities for descriptive purposes:
- controlling access to IRAs;
- organizing and maintaining IRA files;
- monitoring contributions;
- making distributions; and
- complying with reporting requirements.

All of these activities are important because they are either directly or indirectly mandated by IRA law and the IRS as fiduciary responsibilities of IRA trustees.

Controlling Access to IRAs

Financial institutions generally use two main procedures for limiting the IRA participants' access to IRAs. First, some institutions establish account numbering systems for IRAs that differentiate IRAs from other types of deposit accounts and certificates. While the numbering format may be the same as that for other types of accounts, special distinctions in the account numbers for IRAs are usually made. For example, some institutions adopt a separate series of numbers or add a distinctive digit or number to the end of the account number for IRAs, such as –1234-6 or –1234-I. Some institutions further designate IRAs by assigning a distinct set of numbers for each type of IRA.

Account numbering systems that clearly identify IRAs help prevent unauthorized transactions. For example, IRA account designations can signal tellers to take additional precautions before completing a transaction. With data processing systems, special IRA codes can trigger terminal locking mechanisms so that a transaction cannot be posted to the computer. More sophisticated systems use codes to instruct tellers to seek assistance from a supervisor. Whatever the signaling mechanism, alerted tellers should direct IRA participants to the appropriate personnel who are able to identify the participant and determine if the IRA transaction is allowable. All IRA transactions are screened and only allowable transactions by IRA participants are authorized.

The second method financial institutions use to minimize the danger of unauthorized IRA transactions is to retain the passbook, certificate or other evidence of deposit in the participant's file at the institution. As trustee, the financial institution holds legal title to the account and is permitted to retain custody of the evidence of trust assets.

All transactions must then be made with the assistance of IRA specialists, who can guard against excess contributions, premature distributions and prohibited transactions. Under this system, an IRA participant who wants to complete any IRA transaction must first consult the appropriate IRA personnel. Allowable IRA transactions can be authorized and completed according to the participant's wishes, while reasons behind nonallowable transactions can be explained to the customer.

Organizing and Maintaining Files

One reason for creating and maintaining good filing systems for IRAs is that financial institutions acting as IRA trustees must keep records for each participant that show all of the transactions made to the account.[6] Orderly and systematized IRA plan files assure adequate administrative control, hold down administrative costs and minimize the likelihood of errors. Often the IRA plan files are centralized at the institution's main office, with information filed in the new accounts department, in the teller files and within computer storage systems.

The IRA plan files may consist of folders or microfilm records, one for each IRA participant. The files generally contain all the relevant information pertaining to every IRA the institution maintains. Frequently, they are kept in alphabetical order according to the participants' last names and contain the following information:

- a signed trust account agreement (such as Form 5305 or Form 5305-A);
- designation of beneficiary and any change of beneficiary forms;
- all correspondence between the participant and the institution regarding the IRA;
- records of contributions and distributions;
- any so-called "cover your institution" protective liability documentation (Documentation might be warranted whenever an IRA participant requests something unusual. The document could state that the customer was told of possible ramifications and be signed by the customer.);
- copies of report forms sent to the participant and/or the government.

If the institution maintains control of the passbooks and/or certificates of deposit, these are also stored or microfilmed for the participant's file.

For rollover contributions, the file will include copies of the check or other instrument that shows the amount rolled over and the source of the rollover funds. This information is retained in order to answer any questions that might arise about a participant's eligibility to make a rollover contribution.

To insure that all the required procedures have been duly completed, some financial institutions use an IRA checklist, such as the one shown in Figure 4-8. This checklist is included in the participant's file, and it is used to record the completion of various tasks required for the opening of the IRA. It is also used to record subsequent contributions.

As an additional refinement, a tab or index may be used to reference each IRA file. The tab may

FIGURE 4-8
IRA Checklist

IRA CHECKLIST

This form must accompany all new accounts.

Plan Number _____ Account Number _____

Date _____ Opened By _____

Customer's Name _____

Check One: _____ New IRA Plan

_____ New Account with Existing IRA
Number of IRA accounts _____

Check One: _____ Regular (Contributory) IRA

_____ Regular Rollover IRA

_____ Transfer Rollover

_____ Non-Working Spouse IRA

Check the following procedures as they are completed:

_____ Hold Code

_____ 5305 Trust Agreements (2)

_____ Signature Card

_____ Computer Entry Form

_____ Designation of Beneficiary

_____ Disclosure Statement

_____ Remittance of Contribution

_____ Copies to Participant

IRA Administrator _____ Date _____

*A signature card, short name card and hold code are the only forms completed when a second account is opened. Same plan number; new account number.

include the participant's name, address and social security number; the IRA plan and account number; and the year in which the participant will reach the age of 70½. Users of IRA plan files find that a tab or index system provides a thumbnail sketch of a participant that is useful for quick reference.

Monitoring Contributions

During each taxable year, a financial institution must monitor every IRA participant's contributions to an IRA account held by that institution. IRA contributions may be made directly by the participant or indirectly by automatic transfers from other accounts, automatic deposits from a payroll savings plan or preauthorized Transmatic® payment plans.[7] As trustees, institutions cannot knowingly accept excess contributions, as defined by the IRA law. For example, an institution cannot accept a $2,500 IRA contribution. However, institutions are not required to monitor the amount of a participant's income to make sure it is at least the amount of the contribution; this is the participant's responsibility. Many institutions monitor IRA contributions with computer programs that are activated whenever a transaction to an IRA account is completed. Also, special hold codes may be used for IRAs to alert tellers not to complete an IRA transaction until the appropriate authorization is obtained.

Before teller supervisors or IRA specialists who are responsible for monitoring IRA contribution amounts can authorize an IRA deposit, they must verify the total amount deposited to the IRA earlier for the same taxable year. The supervisor or IRA specialist may inspect the deposit amounts posted to the passbook or recorded by hand in the

IRA plan file to determine if the maximum contribution limit has been reached. In an on-line computer system, deposit data may be obtained by direct inquiry on the computer terminal. After receiving authorization to proceed with the transaction, tellers post the deposit to the participant's account.

Between January 1 and April 15, tellers may need to enter the previous taxable year into the computer so that the contributions made for the previous year can be credited properly and the institution can accurately monitor a single year's contribution amount.

As a service to IRA customers, some financial institutions conduct year-end mailings or telephone campaigns to remind all IRA participants of the leeway period for making contributions. These notifications also serve to provide other information regarding customers' IRAs.

Making Distributions

As IRA trustees, financial institutions must exercise care in determining and allowing distributions from IRAs. To meet their fiduciary responsibilities, institutions must carry out special procedures to protect IRA participants from unknowingly engaging in transactions that can lead to tax penalties.

Of primary concern are the areas of premature distribution, underdistribution and overdistribution. Because these actions can lead to tax penalties for IRA participants, financial institutions adopt several administrative measures to minimize the possibility of premature distributions and schedule distributions accurately according to established formulas and life expectancy tables to avoid underdistribution. Financial institutions should also alert participants of the excess distribution tax penalties that would apply if they were to withdraw large amounts.

In order to begin taking distributions, the participant completes the required forms. Any one of the three distribution options described in Chapter 3 may be chosen for taking distributions:
- period certain payments;
- lump-sum payment; or
- life annuity.

Since financial institutions are not permitted to offer life annuities (only life insurance companies can) and lump-sum distributions are fairly straightforward since they involve only a single distribution, this section concentrates on the more complicated option, period certain payments. Recall that the period certain option involves a predetermined length of time.

Distribution Forms and Procedures

Some financial institutions have created a special withdrawal form for use by IRA participants requesting distributions. Information on a typical withdrawal form includes the reason for the withdrawal, the amount withdrawn, the date, the IRA plan and account numbers, and the participant's signature and address. The participant's notification of rights to elect whether or not the institution should withhold taxes from the distribution may be included on the withdrawal form or given as a separate notice. Recall Chapter 3's discussion of how frequently the withholding election notice must be given to participants. Also known as distribution forms, these documents are not specifically required by the IRA law. Consequently, the use of special withdrawal forms is a matter of institution policy.

After any necessary withdrawal forms are completed, distribution checks are authorized by appropriate institution personnel and the transactions are recorded properly. Usually, institutions maintain a record of the date, the check number, the amount of the distribution and the initials of the person who completed the transaction. This record is then kept in the participant's IRA plan file for future reference, along with a copy of the distribution check.

Declaration of intention. Recall that the IRA law requires participants to complete a declaration of intention before any premature distributions can be made. Although the format can be varied, this declaration must state the participant's reason for the withdrawal and must be signed by the participant receiving the distribution. One type of declaration format is reproduced in Figure 4-9.

Notification. If a participant is not yet taking distributions one year prior to the year in which the participant will attain age 70½, some financial institutions send a notice as a reminder that the time is nearing for a decision on how to distribute the assets in the IRA. These optional notifications typically urge participants to consult a tax advisor or an attorney to learn of the distribution options and their tax implications before visiting the institution to establish a distribution schedule.

Distribution agreement. An IRA participant who has decided upon the distribution method must sign a distribution agreement. One example of a distribution agreement, called a benefit election

Chapter Four 153

FIGURE 4-9
Withdrawal/Benefit Election Form

**INDIVIDUAL RETIREMENT
WITHDRAWAL/BENEFIT ELECTION**

File or Account No. _____

Grantor: _____ S/S No.: _____ Date of Birth: _____
Claimant Information (if other than grantor):
Name _____ S/S No.: _____ Date of Birth: _____

TYPE OF WITHDRAWAL OR BENEFIT CLAIM
- ☐ Premature Distribution
- ☐ Rollover
- ☐ Disability Benefit[1]
- ☐ Death Benefit[2]
- ☐ Prohibited Transaction
- ☐ Other _____
- ☐ Normal Distributions Benefit
- ☐ Excess Contributions Refunded Plus Earnings on Such Contributions
- ☐ Transfers to IRA for Spouse Due to Divorce[3]

[1]Medical Certification of Disability Required Prior to Payment of Benefit.
[2]Death Certificate or Other Evidence of Death Required Prior to Payment of Benefit
[3]Pursuant to divorce decree or written instrument incident to divorce.

RETIREMENT ELECTION*
- ☐ PERIOD CERTAIN PAYMENTS (over a period certain not extending beyond the grantor's life expectancy or the joint and last survivor expectancy of the grantor and spouse, if married.) Period Certain: _____
(years, months, etc.)

  Payments to be made: ☐ Monthly ☐ Quarterly ☐ Semiannually ☐ Annually
- ☐ SINGLE SUM PAYMENT (This option may be exercised at any time even though retirement distributions may have commenced pursuant to the period certain option above or "other" option below.)
- ☐ LIFE ANNUITY to be purchased from the_____
(Insurance or Annuity Company)
- ☐ OTHER _____
(Describe, e.g., Interest Only; Irregular as Needed; Partial Single Sum Plus Periodic Payments)

DEATH BENEFIT ELECTION*
- ☐ SINGLE SUM
- ☐ PERIODIC PAYMENTS over_____ years (not to exceed 5 years after death of grantor or grantor's surviving spouse).
- ☐ Other _____
(Note: Use this space to describe any other option permitted by law or regulation, including any option available **only** as to grantor's surviving spouse.)

WITHHOLDING ELECTION
Notice of Withholding on Distributions From IRA's
The distributions you receive from your IRA are subject to Federal income tax withholding unless you elect not to have withholding apply. You may elect not to have withholding apply to your distribution payments by executing the election appearing above the line for your signature on this withdrawal/benefit election form. If you do not execute the election receipt of your payments may be delayed and Federal income tax will be withheld from your distribution at a rate of 10 percent. If you elect not to have withholding apply to your distribution, payments, or if you do not have enough Federal income tax withheld from your (distribution) you may be responsible for payment of estimated tax. You may incur penalties under the estimated tax rules if your withholding and estimated tax payments are not sufficient.

I hereby acknowledge receipt of the Notice of Withholding and ☐ do ☐ do not elect withholding.

I understand that the elections made in this document may not be revoked or changed except by written directions to the Trustee submitted on an amended election form or other form acceptable to the Trustee.

_____   _____   _____
(Signature of Claimant)   Claimant Identity (e.g. grantor, spouse, executor, beneficiary, etc.)   (Date)

For Trustee's Internal Use Only:
1. Payments to begin: _____;
   ☐ Paid by Check; ☐ Transfer to Acct. # _____
2. Additional Comments: _____
   _____

*Annual benefits received must meet the minimum distribution requirements under IRC Section 4974 or a 50% penalty may be imposed by IRS.

SAF Systems and Forms 11515 (Rev. 1/84)   © 1984 United States League of Savings Institutions form, also is shown in Figure 4-9. Although IRA laws do not require a set format, these agreements typically will include the date, the participant's signature and address, and a statement indicating the amount to be distributed and the manner of distribution.

Calculating Minimum Payment Amounts
Life expectancy tables are used to calculate minimum payment amounts. Period certain payments may be made for *not more than* the participant's life expectancy (or the joint and last survivor expectancy of the participant and spouse) (see Chapter 3). However, period certain payments can be made over a period of time that is *less than* the life expectancy. Life expectancy is determined by using actuarial tables approved by the Internal Revenue Service. Figure 4-10 is an IRS-approved table for figuring the life expectancy of an individual participant and Figure 4-11 is an IRS-approved table for figuring the life expectancy of the last survivor of two lives (participant and spouse). Recall from Chapter 3 that the IRS recently approved updated actuarial tables. These updated tables allow participants to withdraw smaller amounts over a longer period of time than did the tables they replaced. The reason smaller distributions are permitted is that the new tables have larger multiples, reflecting more current mortality statistics than the old tables did. Also the new unisex tables apply to all participants. Men and women no longer refer to separate life expectancy tables to determine their required minimum distribution.

The case of Tom Murphy illustrates how the life expectancy tables can be used to establish distribution schedules. Tom, who is 68 years of age, is

FIGURE 4-10
IRS-Approved Unisex Annuity Table

Age	Multiple	Age	Multiple	Age	Multiple
5	76.6	42	40.6	79	10.0
6	75.6	43	39.6	80	9.5
7	74.7	44	38.7	81	8.9
8	73.7	45	37.7	82	8.4
9	72.7	46	36.8	83	7.9
10	71.7	47	35.9	84	7.4
11	70.7	48	34.9	85	6.9
12	69.7	49	34.0	86	6.5
13	68.8	50	33.1	87	6.1
14	67.8	51	32.2	88	5.7
15	66.8	52	31.3	89	5.3
16	65.8	53	30.4	90	5.0
17	64.8	54	29.5	91	4.7
18	63.9	55	28.6	92	4.4
19	62.9	56	27.7	93	4.1
20	61.9	57	26.8	94	3.9
21	60.9	58	25.9	95	3.7
22	59.9	59	25.0	96	3.4
23	59.0	60	24.2	97	3.2
24	58.0	61	23.3	98	3.0
25	57.0	62	22.5	99	2.8
26	56.0	63	21.6	100	2.7
27	55.1	64	20.8	101	2.5
28	54.1	65	20.0	102	2.3
29	53.1	66	19.2	103	2.1
30	52.2	67	18.4	104	1.9
31	51.2	68	17.6	105	1.8
32	50.2	69	16.8	106	1.6
33	49.3	70	16.0	107	1.4
34	48.3	71	15.3	108	1.3
35	47.3	72	14.6	109	1.1
36	46.4	73	13.9	110	1.0
37	45.4	74	13.2	111	.9
38	44.4	75	12.5	112	.8
39	43.5	76	11.9	113	.7
40	42.5	77	11.2	114	.6
41	41.5	78	10.6	115	.5

FIGURE 4-11
IRS-Approved Life Expectancy Table for Last Survivor of Two Lives (Illustrative Portion)

Ages	65	66	67	68	69	70	71	72	73	74
65	25.0	24.6	24.2	23.8	23.4	23.1	22.8	22.5	22.2	22.0
66	24.6	24.1	23.7	23.3	22.9	22.5	22.2	21.9	21.6	21.4
67	24.2	23.7	23.2	22.8	22.4	22.0	21.7	21.3	21.0	20.8
68	23.8	23.3	22.8	22.3	21.9	21.5	21.2	20.8	20.5	20.2
69	23.4	22.9	22.4	21.9	21.5	21.1	20.7	20.3	20.0	19.6
70	23.1	22.5	22.0	21.5	21.1	20.6	20.2	19.8	19.4	19.1
71	22.8	22.2	21.7	21.2	20.7	20.2	19.8	19.4	19.0	18.6
72	22.5	21.9	21.3	20.8	20.3	19.8	19.4	18.9	18.5	18.2
73	22.2	21.6	21.0	20.5	20.0	19.4	19.0	18.5	18.1	17.7
74	22.0	21.4	20.8	20.2	19.6	19.1	18.6	18.2	17.7	17.3
75	21.8	21.1	20.5	19.9	19.3	18.8	18.3	17.8	17.3	16.9
76	21.6	20.9	20.3	19.7	19.1	18.5	18.0	17.5	17.0	16.5
77	21.4	20.7	20.1	19.4	18.8	18.3	17.7	17.2	16.7	16.2
78	21.2	20.5	19.9	19.2	18.6	18.0	17.5	16.9	16.4	15.9
79	21.1	20.4	19.7	19.0	18.4	17.8	17.2	16.7	16.1	15.6
80	21.0	20.2	19.5	18.9	18.2	17.6	17.0	16.4	15.9	15.4
81	20.8	20.1	19.4	18.7	18.1	17.4	16.8	16.2	15.7	15.1
82	20.7	20.0	19.3	18.6	17.9	17.3	16.6	16.0	15.5	14.9
83	20.6	19.9	19.2	18.5	17.8	17.1	16.5	15.9	15.3	14.7
84	20.5	19.8	19.1	18.4	17.7	17.0	16.3	15.7	15.1	14.5
85	20.5	19.7	19.0	18.3	17.6	16.9	16.2	15.6	15.0	14.4
86	20.4	19.6	18.9	18.2	17.5	16.8	16.1	15.5	14.8	14.2
87	20.4	19.6	18.8	18.1	17.4	16.7	16.0	15.4	14.7	14.1
88	20.3	19.5	18.8	18.0	17.3	16.6	15.9	15.3	14.6	14.0
89	20.3	19.5	18.7	18.0	17.2	16.5	15.8	15.2	14.5	13.9
90	20.2	19.4	18.7	17.9	17.2	16.5	15.8	15.1	14.5	13.8

trying to decide how to take withdrawals from his IRA.

Figure 4-10 indicates that at age 68 Tom can, on an actuarial basis, be expected to live another 17.6 years. The proceeds in his IRA may be then distributed to him in equal installments over the next 17.6 years. Although Tom may live past the age of 85 (68 + 17.6 = 85.6), his entire IRA could be

Chapter Four

Ages	65	66	67	68	69	70	71	72	73	74
91	20.2	19.4	18.6	17.9	17.1	16.4	15.7	15.0	14.4	13.7
92	20.2	19.4	18.6	17.8	17.1	16.4	15.7	15.0	14.3	13.7
93	20.1	19.3	18.6	17.8	17.1	16.3	15.6	14.9	14.3	13.6
94	20.1	19.3	18.5	17.8	17.0	16.3	15.6	14.9	14.2	13.6
95	20.1	19.3	18.5	17.8	17.0	16.3	15.6	14.9	14.2	13.5
96	20.1	19.3	18.5	17.7	17.0	16.2	15.5	14.8	14.2	13.5
97	20.1	19.3	18.5	17.7	17.0	16.2	15.5	14.8	14.1	13.5
98	20.1	19.3	18.5	17.7	16.9	16.2	15.5	14.8	14.1	13.4
99	20.0	19.2	18.5	17.7	16.9	16.2	15.5	14.7	14.1	13.4
100	20.0	19.2	18.4	17.7	16.9	16.2	15.4	14.7	14.0	13.4
101	20.0	19.2	18.4	17.7	16.9	16.1	15.4	14.7	14.0	13.3
102	20.0	19.2	18.4	17.6	16.9	16.1	15.4	14.7	14.0	13.3
103	20.0	19.2	18.4	17.6	16.9	16.1	15.4	14.7	14.0	13.3
104	20.0	19.2	18.4	17.6	16.9	16.1	15.4	14.7	14.0	13.3
105	20.0	19.2	18.4	17.6	16.8	16.1	15.4	14.6	13.9	13.3
106	20.0	19.2	18.4	17.6	16.8	16.1	15.3	14.6	13.9	13.3
107	20.0	19.2	18.4	17.6	16.8	16.1	15.3	14.6	13.9	13.2
108	20.0	19.2	18.4	17.6	16.8	16.1	15.3	14.6	13.9	13.3
109	20.0	19.2	18.4	17.6	16.8	16.1	15.3	14.6	13.9	13.2
110	20.0	19.2	18.4	17.6	16.8	16.1	15.3	14.6	13.9	13.3
111	20.0	19.2	18.4	17.6	16.8	16.0	15.3	14.6	13.9	13.2
112	20.0	19.2	18.4	17.6	16.8	16.0	15.3	14.6	13.9	13.3
113	20.0	19.2	18.4	17.6	16.8	16.0	15.3	14.6	13.9	13.2
114	20.0	19.2	18.4	17.6	16.8	16.0	15.3	14.6	13.9	13.2
115	20.0	19.2	18.4	17.6	16.8	16.0	15.3	14.6	13.9	13.2

distributed to him during the 17.6-year life expectancy period, unless he asked the institution to recheck the table each year. (See Chapter 3's discussion of distribution options.) By rechecking the table each year, called annual recalculation, Tom would not be required to deplete his entire IRA balance until age 115. Tom may choose to use the current multiple by having his IRA sponsor recheck the table each year or he may choose to take distributions faster than is required by dividing his IRA balance by a lower multiple than the table indicates.

Another case concerns Jane and Greg Rightman, who are 65 and 69, respectively. Jane decides to receive distributions from her IRA over her own and her husband's joint life expectancy. Figure 4-11 is used to determine joint life expectancies. Jane's age, 65, appears in the vertical column and Greg's age, 69, appears in the horizontal row. The point of intersection indicates their joint life expectancy is 23.4 years. Therefore, substantially equal distributions could be made over 23.4 or fewer years. Jane and Greg could also decide to recheck the table every year and use the then-current multiple. Annual recalculation would allow the Rightmans to deplete Jane's IRA over a period longer than 23.4 years.

To determine the required minimum distribution, the trustee must divide the entire amount in the IRA at the beginning of each year (after the participant reaches age 70½) by the number of years remaining of the participant's life expectancy according to IRS-approved tables. Since the funds in the account continue to earn interest, a yearly calculation by this method results in later payment amounts' differing from the early ones. Although the payments in later years are not equal or even approximately equal to earlier payments, such a means of distribution meets the minimum distribution requirements.

Distributions may be based on the joint life expectancy of a participant and a nonspouse beneficiary. However, the life expectancy multiple to be used for determining the required minimum distribution in these cases can be no greater than 26.2

when the participant reaches age 70. Also, for every year that the participant lives past age 70, the multiple decreases to conform with the minimum distribution incidental benefit requirement. Participants who wish to take distributions in this manner should be advised to consult an attorney or reliable tax advisor.

Another common way to calculate distribution amounts is to use a straight amortization method —as if the institution were repaying an installment loan to the IRA participant. Because interest continues to accumulate on the IRA funds not yet distributed, the payout of accumulated interest is figured into the calculations. This method produces equal payment amounts over the period certain.

After the amount of an annual distribution has been determined, the IRA should be reviewed each year to check that the minimum payout has been made. Because of the severe underdistribution penalty, many financial institutions think it prudent to follow a policy of distributing amounts slightly higher than those calculated from the amortization tables (for example, $215 rather than $211.67).

Federal Income Tax Withholding
IRA participants can elect to have the trustee withhold federal income taxes from their distributions. Institutions making distributions must notify participants of the right to make the election. Institutions must furnish the participant with IRS Form W-4P or a substitute Form W-4P to make this withholding election.

If distributions are in scheduled periodic payments at least as frequently as quarterly, institutions must notify participants of the election of withholding taxes at least once during each calendar year. Notices must be given no earlier than six months before and no later than the date of the first payment. For scheduled periodic payments, the amount withheld is based on tables constructed by the U.S. Treasury. If distributions are less frequent than quarterly or are nonperiodic (payable on demand), notices are given at the time of each distribution.

With nonperiodic distributions, the amount withheld is 10% of the distribution. If the participant does not elect out of withholding, the financial institution trustee must withhold 10% of the distribution.

Once the participant makes a withholding election, it is valid until canceled. A participant may cancel an election at any time by signing another W-4P or a substitute W-4P.

After funds for income tax have been withheld from an IRA distribution, the institution must report this to the IRS and send the funds to a federal depository bank. The institution must make quarterly reports to the IRS on either Form 941, also used for the institution's payroll, or Form 941-E, used only for IRA distributions. These funds are sent to a federal depository bank with Form 8109. The IRS determines how frequently funds withheld must be deposited based on the amounts involved.

Distributions to Beneficiaries
On the death of an IRA participant, a financial institution must execute its fiduciary responsibility by protecting the account funds and properly

remitting them to the correct beneficiary or beneficiaries. To assure that the grantor's wishes are followed, institutions often require a certified copy of the participant's death certificate. In addition, the beneficiaries often are required to submit proper identification to show that they are, in fact, the persons named on the designation of beneficiary form. Both the death certificate and proper identification must be obtained before the institution may release funds from the deceased participant's IRA. Institutions in some states also require an inheritance tax release form, obtained from a state office, before paying funds to a beneficiary.

Complying with Reporting Requirements

As part of their fiduciary responsibilities, institutions must report certain information to the IRS, Social Security Administration and IRA participants by specific dates. The institution reports contributions to the IRS and distributions to the IRS and the Social Security Administration. Regulations require that such IRA reporting be done on magnetic media if more than 250 forms are to be filed with the IRS or Social Security Administration. The institution also sends participants an annual statement and copies of the forms it submitted to the IRS and Social Security Administration. The participant reports IRA activity when completing his or her income tax return. Institutions also may prepare other optional reports to aid their own administration of IRAs.

Institution Reporting for Contributions

Institutions use Form 5498 to report participants' contributions. Form 5498 has separate sections concerning the following:
- regular IRA contributions;

- SEP contributions;
- amounts contributed during the leeway period (January 1 through April 15) that were designated for the previous tax year;
- rollover contributions; and
- any amounts allocable to the cost of life insurance.

Form 5498 is due to the IRS by May 31 for the previous tax year for all IRA plans, regardless of whether or not contributions or other activities occurred. It is possible that the IRS may require additional information in the future.

The following sequence of events shows how the IRS and the participant use information reported by the institution on Form 5498:

1. The customer makes an IRA deposit.
2. The institution records the amount, the type of deposit and the tax year for which it applies.
3. The institution generates a Form 5498 and sends a copy to the IRS.
4. The customer claims an income tax deduction, or lists nondeductible contributions, on his or her federal income tax return Form 1040 or 1040A.
5. The IRS can compare the 1040 or 1040A with the 5498 to verify contributions.

Institution Reporting for Distributions

Institutions report lump-sum distributions to the IRS by the use of Form 1099R. Partial distributions are reported to the Social Security Administration on Form W-2P. A copy of the 1099R or W-2P also is sent to the participant. The purpose of these reports is to enable the participant to determine the taxable amount of the distribution and the IRS to compare the customer's tax return to the amount reported by the institution.

Lump-sum distributions on Form 1099R to the IRS. Institutions complete the following four sections of Form 1099R:
- the institution's (payer's) name, address and federal identifying number;
- the participant's (recipient's) name, address and Social Security (identification) number;
- the amount of the distribution; and
- the code number indicating the reason (category) for the distribution.

The code numbers for indicating the reason for distribution are four-digit numbers starting with 555. The fourth digit identifies the reasons as follows:
- 1—a premature distribution other than rollover, disability or death
- 2—a rollover
- 3—disability
- 4—death
- 6—other
- 7—normal distribution
- 8—excess contributions refunded plus earnings thereon (for excess contributions that were made and withdrawn in the same year)
- P—prior year (to indicate tax treatment of earnings on excess contributions that were made in the year just prior to the year of distribution)

When excess contributions are withdrawn, the total distribution and the earnings on the excess are reported separately. The digit 8 is used when the earnings are taxable in the same year that they are withdrawn. The letter P is used when such earnings are reportable for the previous tax year. The Form 1099R is shown in Figure 4-12.

Institutions must file Copy A of Form 1099R with

FIGURE 4-12
Form 1099-R

9898 ☐ VOID ☐ CORRECTED For Official Use Only

Type or machine print PAYER'S name, street address, city, state, and ZIP code		1 Amount includible as income (Add Boxes 2 and 3) $ 2 Capital gain (For lump-sum distributions only) $	OMB No. 1545-0119 1987 Statement for Recipients of	**Total Distributions From Profit-Sharing, Retirement Plans, Individual Retirement Arrangements, Insurance Contracts, Etc.**
PAYER'S Federal identification number	RECIPIENT'S identification number	3 Ordinary income $	4 Federal income tax withheld $	**Copy A For Internal Revenue Service Center** For Paperwork Reduction Act Notice and instructions for completing this form, see Instructions for Forms 1099, 1098, 5498, 1096, and W-2G.
Type or machine print RECIPIENT'S name (first, middle, last)		5 Employee contributions or insurance premiums $	6 Net unrealized appreciation in employer's securities $	
Street address		7 Category of distribution	8 IRA or SEP distributions $	
City, state, and ZIP code		9 Other $ %	10 State income tax withheld $	
Account number (optional)		Payer's state number	Your percentage of total distribution %	

Form **1099-R** 13-2581759 **Do NOT Cut or Separate Forms on This Page** Department of the Treasury - Internal Revenue Service

the IRS by the end of February for the previous taxable year. Copy B is sent to IRA participants by the end of January.

Partial distributions on Form W-2P to the Social Security Administration. Partial or periodic distributions are reported on Form W-2P, entitled "Statement for Recipients of Annuities, Pensions, Retired Pay, or IRA Payments" as shown in Figure 4-13. Although the format of the W-2P appears different from the 1099R, basically the same information is required from the institution, and the same code numbers are used on both forms.

Form W-2P also has two parts. Copy A must be filed with the Social Security Administration by the end of February and Copy B must be received by IRA participants by the end of January following

FIGURE 4-13
Form W-2P

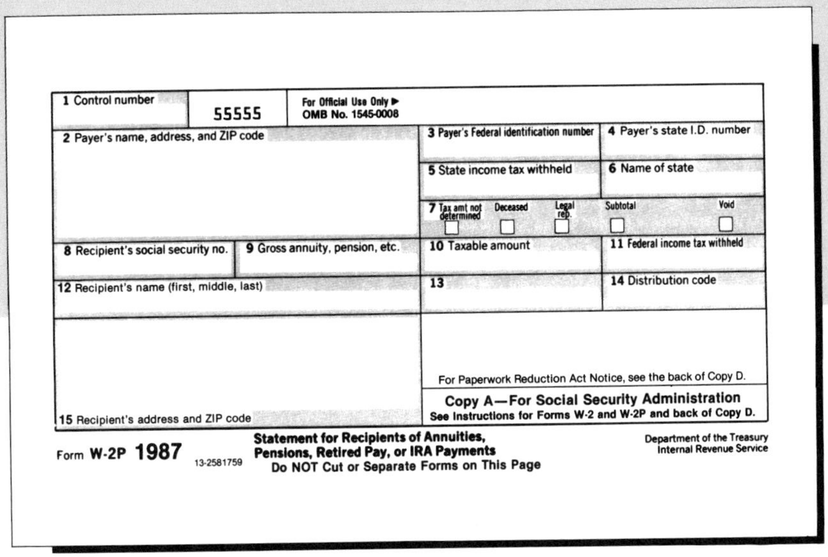

1 Control number 55555
For Official Use Only ▶ OMB No. 1545-0008
2 Payer's name, address, and ZIP code
3 Payer's Federal identification number
4 Payer's state I.D. number
5 State income tax withheld
6 Name of state
7 Tax amt not determined ☐ Deceased ☐ Legal rep. ☐ Subtotal ☐ Void ☐
8 Recipient's social security no.
9 Gross annuity, pension, etc.
10 Taxable amount
11 Federal income tax withheld
12 Recipient's name (first, middle, last)
13
14 Distribution code
For Paperwork Reduction Act Notice, see the back of Copy D.
Copy A—For Social Security Administration
See Instructions for Forms W-2 and W-2P and back of Copy D.
15 Recipient's address and ZIP code
Form **W-2P 1987** 13-2581759
Statement for Recipients of Annuities, Pensions, Retired Pay, or IRA Payments
Do NOT Cut or Separate Forms on This Page
Department of the Treasury Internal Revenue Service

the taxable year. The Social Security Administration forwards Copy A to the IRS.

Annual Statements to Participants

Two yearly statements pertaining to IRA account activity are sent to participants. One, called the annual statement, contains essentially the information on Form 5498, shown in Figure 4-14, plus the value of the participant's account at the end of the calendar year. In fact, a copy of Form 5498 may be used as the annual statement if the value of the account is stated on the form. If the annual statement is furnished on a form other than a copy of Form 5498, the following language must appear on the statement: *This information is being furnished to the Internal Revenue Service.* The annual statement must be sent to the IRA account holder by May 31, for the previous calendar year.

The second yearly statement is required by the Tax Reform Act of 1986. This Act requires institutions to provide certain information to both the IRS and each participant by January 31, for the previous calendar year. The IRS may use this statement or report to monitor deductible and nondeductible amounts; however this is not the official purpose for the report. This report must contain the following three facts:
- contributions made to the IRA during the calendar year;
- distributions from the IRA during the calendar year; and
- the account balance as of the end of the calendar year.

Participants' Reporting Responsibilities
Most participants contributing to IRAs are not required to file special forms with the IRS. Participants merely follow the directions on their IRS Form 1040 or 1040A when completing their federal income tax returns. No other filing is required for allowable IRA contributions.

Some IRA participants must file Form 5329, "Return for Individual Retirement Arrangement Taxes," as shown in Figure 4-15. This form is required only when:
- tax penalties are imposed for excess contributions or distributions, premature distributions or insufficient distributions; or
- any activity occurs other than making allowable contributions to or distributions from IRAs.

IRA participants to whom these circumstances apply complete Form 5329 each applicable year

FIGURE 4-14
Form 5498

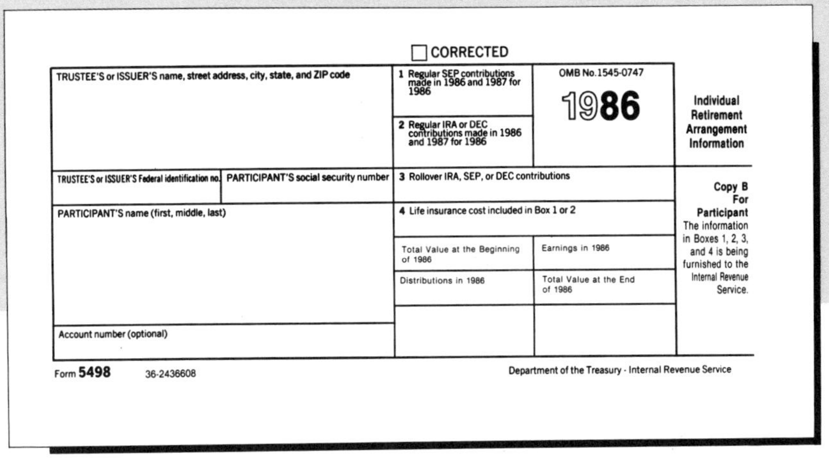

☐ CORRECTED

TRUSTEE'S or ISSUER'S name, street address, city, state, and ZIP code

1 Regular SEP contributions made in 1986 and 1987 for 1986

2 Regular IRA or DEC contributions made in 1986 and 1987 for 1986

OMB No. 1545-0747

1986

Individual Retirement Arrangement Information

TRUSTEE'S or ISSUER'S Federal identification no. | PARTICIPANT'S social security number

3 Rollover IRA, SEP, or DEC contributions

Copy B For Participant
The information in Boxes 1, 2, 3, and 4 is being furnished to the Internal Revenue Service.

PARTICIPANT'S name (first, middle, last)

4 Life insurance cost included in Box 1 or 2

Total Value at the Beginning of 1986 | Earnings in 1986

Distributions in 1986 | Total Value at the End of 1986

Account number (optional)

Form **5498** 36-2436608 Department of the Treasury - Internal Revenue Service

and include this form with their federal income tax returns.

Optional Institution Reports

Additional reports, prepared by the employees administering IRAs or automatically by computer, often are provided to both financial institution management and to IRA participants. The number and type of reports vary according to the needs and policies of each institution.

IRA reports are routinely prepared for an institution's management. These in-house IRA reports serve to provide an overview of IRA activity during a particular period. IRA reports may detail the following activity:

- number of accounts opened and closed;

FIGURE 4-15
Form 5329

Form **5329**	**Return for Individual Retirement Arrangement Taxes**	OMB No. 1545-0203
Department of the Treasury Internal Revenue Service	(Under Sections 408(f), 4973, and 4974 of the Internal Revenue Code) ▶ Attach to Form 1040.	**1986** Attachment Sequence No. **28**

Name | Your social security number

Address (number and street)

City or town, state, and ZIP code

Part I — Excess Contributions Tax for Individual Retirement Arrangements

Complete this part if, either in this year or in earlier years, you have contributed more to your IRA than is or was allowable as a deduction and you have an excess contribution subject to tax.

1. Excess contributions for 1986 (see Instructions for line 1). Do *not* include this amount on Form 1040, line 26 ... **1**
2. Earlier year excess contributions not previously eliminated (see Instructions for line 2) . **2**
3. Contribution credit. (If your maximum allowable deduction for 1986 is more than your actual contribution, see instructions for line 3; otherwise, enter zero.) ... **3**
4a. 1986 distributions out of your account that are taxable income ... **4a**
  b. 1985 tax year excess contributions (if any) withdrawn after the due date (including extensions) of your 1985 income tax return, and 1984 and earlier tax year excess contributions withdrawn in 1986.
   Do *not* enter any withdrawn excess contributions on line 4b in the tax year that the excess contributions were made:
   • your total IRA contributions (other than rollover contributions) were more than $2,250 (or if the total contributions for the year include employer contributions to a SEP, $2,250 increased by the lesser of the amount of the employer contributions to the SEP or $30,000); or
   • you took a deduction for the excess contributions on your Form 1040.
   Instead, enter these withdrawn excess contributions on line 4a of Form 5329 and also on line 16 of Form 1040. **4b**
  c. Add lines 3 through 4b ... **4c**
5. Adjusted earlier year excess contributions (line 2 minus line 4c but not less than zero) ... **5**
6. Total excess contributions (add lines 1 and 5) ... **6**
7. Tax (6% of line 6 or 6% of the value of your IRA on the last day of 1986, whichever is smaller). Enter tax on Form 1040, line 54 **7**

Part II — Tax on Premature Distributions

Complete this part if you received a distribution from your IRA before you reached age 59½. Also, enter the amount of the distribution on Form 1040, line 16.

8a. If you entered into a prohibited transaction as described in the Instructions, borrowed any amount from one of your individual retirement annuities, or pledged any part of your individual retirement annuity contracts, enter 10% of the value of the account or annuity at the beginning of the year ... **8a**
  b. If in 1986 any part of your arrangement was invested in collectibles (see Instructions for line 8b), include 10% of the cost of the collectibles here ... **8b**
9. Enter 10% of the amount of the premature distributions from your arrangement during the year (see Instructions for line 9 for items that are not considered taxable distributions) ... **9**
10. Enter 10% of the amount from your individual retirement savings accounts that you pledged as security for a loan **10**
11. Total tax (add lines 8a through 10). Enter here and on Form 1040, line 54 ... **11**

Part III — Tax on Excess Accumulation in Individual Retirement Accounts and Annuities

12. Tax based on current year distribution method (see worksheet in Instructions) ... **12**
13. Tax based on aggregate distribution method (see worksheet in Instructions) ... **13**
14. Tax due. Enter amount from line 12 or, if aggregate distribution method is applicable, enter the smaller of line 12 or line 13. Also include this amount on Form 1040, line 54 ... **14**

Please Sign Here — Under penalties of perjury, I declare that I have examined this return, including accompanying schedules and statements, and to the best of my knowledge and belief, it is true, correct, and complete. Declaration of preparer (other than taxpayer) is based on all information of which preparer has any knowledge.

Your signature _____ Date _____

Paid Preparer's Use Only

Preparer's signature		Date	Check if self-employed ▶ ☐	Preparer's social security no.
Firm's name (or yours, if self-employed) and address			E.I. No. ▶	
			ZIP code ▶	

For Paperwork Reduction Act Notice, see page 1 of Instructions.   Form **5329** (1986)

- source of new account funds;
- amount of contributions;
- amount of distributions; and
- interest earned.

Some financial institutions send annual letters to inform IRA participants of general information about their IRAs and to provide specific details and instructions. For example, a letter can be enclosed with the annual statement to participants to inform them of any new regulations concerning eligibility, contribution or distribution procedures, or any new deposit options an institution might offer for IRAs. Such a letter might also advise IRA participants to check the reported data on the annual statement against their own records for agreement. IRA and retirement information also may be included in newsletters or other customer service publications.

Summary

By offering IRAs, a financial institution takes on the responsibility of the IRA trustee or custodian. An institution should consider how to handle these responsibilities before offering IRAs. An institution should adopt a trust account agreement which specifies the institution as trustee and the participant as grantor. A formal, written statement should be developed detailing the terms and conditions of the IRA deposit options the institution plans to offer. Once these preparations have been made, the institution may begin to offer IRAs.

Specific duties employees have with IRAs depend upon the size of the institution, the number of IRAs that are opened and how the IRA function is

organized. In most institutions, new accounts employees are responsible for opening IRAs. Opening an IRA requires four basic steps:
1. introduce the concepts of IRAs to the prospective participant;
2. describe the IRA deposit options offered by the institution;
3. execute the required documents and furnish copies to the participant; and
4. conduct follow-up programs.

When an IRA is opened, the following four documents must be prepared and given to the account holder:
- trust account agreement, also called the plan agreement;
- disclosure statement;
- designation of beneficiary; and
- deposit information.

In addition to these required documents, institutions may use additional documentation that aids their administrative duties.

Necessary administrative procedures for existing IRAs can be grouped into the following five major activities for descriptive purposes:
- controlling access to IRAs;
- organizing and maintaining IRA files;
- monitoring contributions;
- making distributions; and
- complying with reporting requirements.

All of these activities are important because they are either directly or indirectly mandated by IRA law and the IRS as fiduciary responsibilities of IRA trustees. Figure 4-16 summarizes the IRA reporting requirements for both participants and financial institutions. The chart lists where each form is filed and the deadlines for filing.

FIGURE 4-16
IRA Reporting Requirements

Form	Completed By	Reports	Filed With	Deadline
Annual Statements to Participants	Financial institution	All IRA activity for the preceding calendar year and leeway period	Participants	May 31
TRA-86 Report to participants in any written format	Financial institution	End-of-year balance	Participants	January 31
1099R	Financial institution	Lump-sum distributions	Copy A to IRS Copy B to participants	February 28 January 31
W-2P	Financial institution	Partial or periodic distributions	Copy A to Social Security Copy B to participants	February 28 January 31
5498	Financial institution	All contributions identified by type and the calendar year for which they apply	Copy A to IRS Copy B to participants (as annual statement)	May 31 May 31
5329	IRA participant	Penalty transactions	IRS	April 15 (or extensions granted by the IRS)

Chapter Questions

1. When can a financial institution legally be held liable for a breach of fiduciary responsibility?
2. Describe some basic provisions of an IRA trust account agreement.
3. List the required and optional forms used to open an IRA.
4. Explain the purpose of an IRA disclosure statement. List any four required disclosures of the regulatory section and any four required disclosures of the financial section.
5. In what two ways can a financial institution control access to IRAs?
6. What are the six items that should be included in a participant's IRA plan file?
7. Describe specifically a financial institution's responsibility for monitoring contributions.
8. Describe the procedure used in your institution for making the following distributions. List any documents required.
   a. allowable distribution (lump-sum)
   b. allowable distribution (period certain payments)
   c. premature distribution (due to financial need)
   d. distribution to beneficiary upon participant's death
9. What are the five IRA reports that financial institutions are required to file? Briefly describe the purposes for filing each.

Footnotes

[1] IRC Sections 1.408, 3405, 6047, 6652, 6693 and 6704
[2] IRC, Section 408(a)
[3] The phrase "material adverse change" is a legal term for any alteration of a specific scope that

affects the disclosure statement. What constitutes such a change is decided by the courts. Therefore, the advice of legal counsel should be sought either when an institution proposes to change its disclosure statement or when the IRA law is amended.

[4]Treasury Regulation Section 1.408-6(d)

[5]FSLIC regulations 564.2(b)(1) and 564.2(b)(2) still apply. However 564.2(b)(3), which required using a signature card, was eliminated.

[6]Home Owners Loan Act of 1933, Title 12, U.S. Code, Sec. 1464, Subsec. 5(1), as amended

[7]Transmatic® is the name of a preauthorized payments system licensed by SAF Systems and Forms, an affiliate of the United States League of Savings Institutions.

Simplified Employee Pension Plans

Chapter Five

Chapter Five
Objectives

After studying this chapter, you should be able to:

- Describe the benefits of a SEP to an employer and an employee;
- Explain how to establish a SEP;
- Explain whom an employer must cover under a SEP;
- List the information that an employer must provide to employees who are eligible to participate in a SEP;
- State the contribution limits for SEPs;
- Explain how a SEP integrated with Social Security would work;
- Describe the benefits of a salary deferral SEP to an employer and an employee; and
- State how much employees and employers may elect to contribute into a salary deferral SEP.

As a result of the Tax Reform Act of 1986, Simplified Employee Pension Plans (SEPs) now have greater tax advantages compared to regular IRAs and are, therefore, likely to become more popular. Because SEPs provide financial institutions with the opportunity to attract deposits in substantial amounts, financial institution employees must become knowledgeable in this area, so that they can provide good customer service to small business owners. This chapter describes what SEPs are, who is eligible to have one, and what rules apply to contributions, deductions and reporting. Also explained are salary deferral SEPs, which the Tax Reform Act of 1986 now permits.

Establishing a SEP

Recall from Chapter 1 that a simplified employee pension plan or SEP is an arrangement by which employers make contributions to eligible employees' IRAs. The Internal Revenue Code Section 408(k) spells out the rules for SEPs.

To establish a SEP, the employer adopts a plan document with any trustee or custodian that offers IRAs. Depending upon the type of plan document used, the employer and employees can choose from various benefit options, such as the percentage of compensation to be contributed and if a Keogh account will be permitted with the SEP.

The employer specifies the eligibility requirements, within those required by law, on the SEP plan document. A commonly used plan document is the IRS Form 5305-SEP (see Figure 5-1). This form is simple to complete. The employer fills in the business name; selects the minimum age and length-of-service eligibility requirements; and checks boxes to include or not include union employees and those who earn less than $300 during the tax year. The last lines are for the employer's signature, date and trustee's signature. The trustee is usually represented by the person who opens the account for the business customer. The remainder of this one page, two-sided document basically consists of instructions for the employer on how the plan works, and information for employees in a question-and-answer format.

A different type of plan document is necessary under certain situations. For instance, the plan described in Form 5305-SEP cannot be used if the employer maintains any other qualified retirement plan or wants to integrate contributions with Social Security. Also, a form 5305-SEP cannot be used to establish a salary deferral SEP. These situations are explained later in this chapter.

Employee Eligibility

Employers, also known as owner-employees, decide the eligibility requirements for participation in a SEP and must follow the same eligibility requirements as all other employees. According to IRA law, under a SEP, contributions for a given calendar year must be made on behalf of every employee who has attained age 21, and has worked for the employer three out of the last five years. The employer can exclude employees who earn less than $300 a year, are covered under a collective bargaining agreement (usually, union membership) and/or are nonresident aliens earning no U.S. income.[1]

Of course, employers may choose to provide benefits to all of their employees regardless of whether or not they have attained a certain age or length of

FIGURE 5-1
Form 5305-SEP, Side 1

Form **5305-SEP**
(Rev. January 1987)
Department of the Treasury
Internal Revenue Service

Simplified Employee Pension-Individual Retirement Accounts Contribution Agreement
(Under Section 408(k) of the Internal Revenue Code)

OMB No. 1545-0499
Expires 10-31-88

Do NOT File with Internal Revenue Service

_____ makes the following agreement under the terms of section 408(k) of
(Business name—employer)
the Internal Revenue Code and the instructions to this form.

The employer agrees to provide for discretionary contributions in each calendar year to the Individual Retirement Accounts or Individual Retirement Annuities (IRA's) of all eligible employees who are at least _____ years old (not over 21 years old) (see instruction "Who May Participate") and worked in at least _____ years (not over 3 years) of the immediately preceding 5 years (see instruction "Who May Participate"). This ☐ includes ☐ does not include employees covered under a collective bargaining agreement and ☐ includes ☐ does not include employees whose total compensation during the year is less than $300.

The employer agrees that contributions made on behalf of each eligible employee will:
- Be made only on the first $200,000 of compensation (as adjusted per Code section 408(k)(3)(C)).
- Be made in an amount that is the same percentage of total compensation for every employee.
- Be limited to the smaller of $30,000 (or if greater, ¼ of the dollar limitation in effect under section 415(b)(1)(A)) or 15% of compensation.
- Be paid to the employee's IRA trustee, custodian, or insurance company (for an annuity contract).

_____   _____
Signature of employer   Date

By _____

Instructions for the Employer
(Section references are to the Internal Revenue Code, unless otherwise noted.)

Paperwork Reduction Act Notice.—The Paperwork Reduction Act of 1980 says we must tell you why we are collecting this information, how it is to be used, and whether you have to give it to us. The information is used to determine if you are entitled to a deduction for contributions made to a SEP. Your completing this form is only required if you want to establish a Model SEP.

Purpose of Form.—Form 5305-SEP (Model SEP) is used by an employer to make an agreement to provide benefits to all employees under a Simplified Employee Pension (SEP) plan described in section 408(k). This form is NOT to be filed with IRS.

What Is a SEP Plan?—A SEP provides an employer with a simplified way to make contributions toward an employee's retirement income. Under a SEP, the employer is permitted to contribute a certain amount (see below) to an employee's Individual Retirement Account or Individual Retirement Annuity (IRA's). The employer makes contributions directly to an IRA set up by an employee with a bank, insurance company, or other qualified financial institution. When using this form to establish a SEP, the IRA must be a model IRA established on an IRS form or a master or prototype IRA for which IRS has issued a favorable opinion letter. Making the agreement on Form 5305-SEP does not establish an employer IRA as described under section 408(c).

This form may not be used by an employer who:
- Currently maintains any other qualified retirement plan.
- Has maintained in the past a defined benefit plan, even if now terminated.
- Has any eligible employees for whom IRA's have not been established.

- Uses the services of leased employees (as described in section 414(n)).
- Is a member of an affiliated service group (as described in section 414(m)), a controlled group of corporations (as described in section 414(b)), or trades or businesses under common control (as described in section 414(c)), UNLESS all eligible employees of all the members of such groups, trades, or businesses, participate under the SEP.
- This form should only be used if the employer will pay the cost of the SEP contributions. This form is not suitable for a SEP that provides for contributions at the election of the employee whether or not made pursuant to a salary reduction agreement.

Who May Participate.—Any employee who is at least 21 years old and has performed "service" for you in at least 3 years of the immediately preceding 5 years must be permitted to participate in the SEP. However, you may establish less restrictive eligibility requirements if you choose. "Service" is any work performed for you for any period of time, however short. Further, if you are a member of an affiliated service group, a controlled group of corporations, or trades or businesses under common control, "service" includes any work performed for any period of time for any other member of such group, trades, or businesses. Generally, to make the agreement, all eligible employees (including all eligible employees, if any, of other members of an affiliated service group, a controlled group of corporations, or trades or businesses under common control) must participate in the plan. However, employees covered under a collective bargaining agreement and certain nonresident aliens may be excluded if section 410(b)(3)(A) or 410(b)(3)(C) applies to them. Employees whose total compensation for the year is less than $300 may be excluded.

Amount of Contributions.—You are not required to make any contributions to an employee's SEP-IRA in a given year. However, if you do make contributions, you must make them to the IRA's of all eligible employees, whether or not they are still employed at the time contributions are made. The contributions made must be the same percentage of each employee's total compensation (up to a maximum compensation base of $200,000 as adjusted per section 408(k)(3)(C) for cost of living changes). The contributions you make in a year for any one employee may not be more than the smaller of $30,000 or 15% of that employee's total compensation (figured without considering the SEP-IRA contributions).

For this purpose, compensation includes:
- Amounts received for personal services actually performed (see section 1.219-1(c) of the Income Tax Regulations); and
- Earned income defined under section 401(c)(2).

In making contributions, you may not discriminate in favor of any employee who is highly compensated.

Under this form you may not integrate your SEP contributions with, or offset them by, contributions made under the Federal Insurance Contributions Act (FICA).

Currently, employers who have established a SEP using this agreement and have provided each participant with a copy of this form, including the questions and answers, are not required to file the annual information returns, Forms 5500, 5500-C, 5500-R, or 5500EZ for the SEP.

Form 5305-SEP, Side 2

Form 5305-SEP (Rev. 1-87)   Page **2**

Deducting Contributions.—You may deduct all contributions to a SEP subject to the limitations of section 404(h). This SEP is maintained on a calendar year basis and contributions to the SEP are deductible for your taxable year with or within which the calendar year ends. Contributions made for a particular taxable year and contributed by the due date of your income tax return (including extensions) shall be deemed made in that taxable year.

Making the Agreement.— This agreement is considered made when (1) IRA's have been established for all of your eligible employees, (2) you have completed all blanks on the agreement form without modification, and (3) you have given all your eligible employees copies of the agreement form, instructions, and questions and answers.

Keep the agreement form with your records; do not file it with IRS.

Information for the Employee

The information provided explains what a Simplified Employee Pension plan is, how contributions are made, and how to treat your employer's contributions for tax purposes.

Please read the questions and answers carefully. For more specific information, also see the agreement form and instructions to your employer on this form.

Questions and Answers

1. Q. What is a Simplified Employee Pension, or SEP?

A. A SEP is a retirement income arrangement under which your employer may contribute any amount each year up to the smaller of $30,000 or 15% of your compensation into **your own** Individual Retirement Account/Annuity (IRA).

Your employer will provide you with a copy of the agreement containing participation requirements and a description of the basis upon which employer contributions may be made to your IRA.

All amounts contributed to your IRA by your employer belong to you, even after you separate from service with that employer.

The $30,000 limitation referred to above may be increased by ¼ of the dollar limitation in effect under section 415(b)(1)(A).

2. Q. Must my employer contribute to my IRA under the SEP?

A. Whether or not your employer makes a contribution to the SEP is entirely within the employer's discretion. If a contribution is made under the SEP, it must be allocated to all the eligible employees according to the SEP agreement. The Model SEP specifies that the contribution on behalf of each eligible employee will be the same percentage of compensation (excluding compensation higher than $200,000) for all employees.

3. Q. How much may my employer contribute to my SEP-IRA in any year?

A. Under the Model SEP (**Form 5305-SEP**) that your employer has adopted, your employer will determine the amount of contribution to be made to your IRA each year. However, the contribution for any year is limited to the smaller of $30,000 or 15% of your compensation for that year. The compensation used to determine this limit does not include any amount which is contributed by your employer to your IRA under the SEP. The agreement does not require an employer to maintain a particular level of contributions. It is possible that for a given year no employer contribution will be made on an employee's behalf.

Also see Question 5.

4. Q. How do I treat my employer's SEP contributions for my taxes?

A. The amount your employer contributes for years beginning after 1986 is excludable from your gross income subject to certain limitations including the lesser of $30,000 or 15% of compensation mentioned in 1.A. above and is not includable as taxable wages on your Form W-2.

5. Q. May I also contribute to my IRA if I am a participant in a SEP?

A. Yes. You may still contribute the lesser of $2,000 or 100% of your compensation to an IRA. However, the amount which is deductible is subject to various limitations.

Also see Question 11.

6. Q. Are there any restrictions on the IRA I select to deposit my SEP contributions in?

A. Under the Model SEP that is approved by IRS, contributions must be made to either a Model IRA which is executed on an IRS form or a master or prototype IRA for which IRS has issued a favorable opinion letter.

7. Q. What if I don't want a SEP-IRA?

A. Your employer may require that you become a participant in such an arrangement as a condition of employment. However, if the employer does not require all eligible employees to become participants and an eligible employee elects not to participate, all other employees of the same employer may be prohibited from entering into a SEP-IRA arrangement with that employer. If one or more eligible employees do not participate and the employer attempts to establish a SEP-IRA agreement with the remaining employees, the resulting arrangement may result in adverse tax consequences to the participating employees.

8. Q. Can I move funds from my SEP-IRA to another tax-sheltered IRA?

A. Yes, it is permissible for you to withdraw, or receive, funds from your SEP-IRA, and no more than 60 days later, place such funds in another IRA, or SEP-IRA. This is called a "rollover" and may not be done without penalty more frequently than at one-year intervals. However, there are no restrictions on the number of times you may make "transfers" if you arrange to have such funds transferred between the trustees, so that you never have possession.

9. Q. What happens if I withdraw my employer's contribution from my IRA?

A. If you don't want to leave the employer's contribution in your IRA, you may withdraw it at any time, but any amount withdrawn is includable in your income. Also, if withdrawals occur before attainment of age 59½, and not on account of death or disability, you may be subject to a penalty tax.

10. Q. May I participate in a SEP even though I'm covered by another plan?

A. An employer may not adopt this IRS Model SEP (**Form 5305-SEP**) if the employer maintains another qualified retirement plan or has ever maintained a qualified defined benefit plan. However, if you work for several employers you may be covered by a SEP of one employer and a different SEP or pension or profit-sharing plan of another employer.

Also see Questions 11 and 12.

11. Q. What happens if too much is contributed to my SEP-IRA in one year?

A. Any contribution that is more than the yearly limitations may be withdrawn without penalty by the due date (plus extensions) for filing your tax return (normally April 15th), but is includable in your gross income. Excess contributions left in your SEP-IRA account after that time are subject to a 6% excise tax. Withdrawals of those contributions may be taxed as premature withdrawals.

Also see Question 10.

12. Q. Do I need to file any additional forms with IRS because I participate in a SEP?

A. No.

13. Q. Is my employer required to provide me with information about SEP-IRA's and the SEP agreement?

A. Yes, your employer must provide you with a copy of the executed SEP agreement (**Form 5305-SEP**), these Questions and Answers, and provide a statement each year showing any contribution to your IRA.

Also see Question 4.

14. Q. Is the financial institution where I establish my IRA also required to provide me with information?

A. Yes, it must provide you with a disclosure statement which contains the following items of information in plain, nontechnical language:

(1) the statutory requirements which relate to IRA;

(2) the tax consequences which follow the exercise of various options and what those options are;

(3) participation eligibility rules, and rules on the deductibility and nondeductibility of retirement savings;

(4) the circumstances and procedures under which you may revoke your IRA, including the name, address, and telephone number of the person designated to receive notice of revocation (**this explanation must be prominently displayed at the beginning of the disclosure statement**);

(5) explanations of when penalties may be assessed against you because of specified prohibited or penalized activities concerning your IRA; and

(6) financial disclosure information which:

(a) either projects value growth rates of your IRA under various contribution and retirement schedules, or describes the method of computing and allocating annual earnings and charges which may be assessed;

(b) describes whether, and for what period, the growth projections for the plan are guaranteed, or a statement of the earnings rate and terms on which the projection is based;

(c) states the sales commission to be charged in each year expressed as a percentage of $1,000; and

(d) states the proportional amount of any nondeductible life insurance which may be a feature of your IRA.

See **Publication 590**, Individual Retirement Arrangements (IRA's), available at most IRS offices, for a more complete explanation of the disclosure requirements.

In addition to this disclosure statement, the financial institution is required to provide you with a financial statement each year. It may be necessary to retain and refer to statements for more than one year in order to evaluate the investment performance of the IRA and in order that you will know how to report IRA distributions for tax purposes.

☆ U.S. Government Printing Office: 1987—181-447/40073

service. The employer also may choose to cover employees who earn less than $300 a year or those who belong to a union provided that such standards are applied uniformly to all employees. And, since the owner-employee must meet the same eligibility requirements that are set for employees, he or she will not want to set age or service requirements that are too stringent. For example, suppose Ron Grimwald, who is 18 years old, opens his own pizza sausage distributorship. He employs only college graduates as salesmen. If Ron establishes a SEP and requires a minimum age of 21 and one year of service for participation, he will have to make contributions for every employee next year. However, Ron will not be eligible to contribute for himself for another three years, until he is 21.

All employees who meet the SEP's eligibility requirements must open IRAs at a financial institution of their choice. If an eligible employee refuses to open an IRA, the IRS gives the employer the authority to establish an IRA for that employee, using the financial institution's usual IRA documentation.[2] An employee also may use his or her existing IRA to receive SEP contributions.

Employer-Provided Information

Depending on the plan that the employer chooses to establish a SEP, the employer must give the employees certain information, as required by both the IRS and the Department of Labor. If Form 5305-SEP is used, the employer must give a copy of the completed form to all eligible employees. If the employer does not use Form 5305-SEP, then all eligible employees must receive a summary of whatever plan has been selected.[3] Basically, if a plan other than the Form 5305-SEP is used, the employee receives the same general information that is found on the Form 5305-SEP along with specific information that explains the particular plan adopted.

The employer must also give each participant an annual statement indicating the amount contributed on his or her behalf. Before 1987, these contributions were included in the employee's gross income and reported on his or her W-2 tax statement. Employees would then deduct the employer contributions made to their IRAs on their Form 1040. However, starting in 1987, contributions made on behalf of the eligible employees are no longer included on their Form W-2 as taxable income. Therefore, employees do not take a deduction for SEP contributions made to their IRAs when filing their income tax returns. To clarify, before 1987, employers reported SEP contribution amounts as income to the employee, and the employee could deduct these amounts. Today SEP contribution amounts are not reported as income to the employee. Therefore, the employer can still deduct SEP contributions made for his or her employees, but there is no tax effect change for employees.

Although employees may open their IRAs to receive SEP contributions at any IRA sponsor, typically they use the same sponsor that established the SEP for their employer. By going elsewhere, they would create additional administrative work for their employer. However, if the employer persuades an employee to choose a *particular* IRA and that IRA restricts the employee's ability to withdraw funds, the employer must provide the employee with two additional pieces of information:
- a written explanation of these restrictions; and
- a statement which indicates that other IRAs (into

which rollovers or employee contributions may be made) may not be subject to such restrictions. To summarize, each participant must receive (in addition to the IRA documents and the annual contribution statement):

- a copy of the executed SEP agreement (or a summary of its key provisions); and
- a copy of the IRS SEP disclosure information statement.

Recall that if the Form 5305-SEP is used, these two items are contained on one double-sided sheet of paper.

Contribution and Deduction Rules

SEP contribution and deduction rules provide many benefits and protections for eligible employees. For example, unlike other employer-sponsored pension plans, employer contributions to a SEP become immediately and fully vested for the employee (100% vested). This means that the employee cannot forfeit or lose the benefit of any contributions that were made on his or her behalf. In addition, an employer may not prohibit an employee from withdrawing funds from the plan or make retention of the funds in the plan a condition of employment. However, all IRA rules do apply once money is contributed under a SEP plan to an IRA.

SEP contributions are determined under a written allocation formula which specifies two things:
- the eligibility requirements for participation; and
- how to compute the amounts to be allocated to employees.

Special SEP provisions prohibit an employer from discriminating in favor of an employee who is an officer, shareholder, self-employed individual or highly compensated. However, the employer can change the formula for contributions or eliminate contributions from year to year.

The following paragraphs list contribution and deduction rules that apply for SEPs. They are grouped according to what and to whom they apply.

SEP Contribution Amounts and Percentages

A SEP allows an employer to make payments to each eligible employee's IRA of up to 15% of an employee's compensation or $30,000, whichever is less. The contribution percentage must be the same for all eligible employees.[4] An employee may contribute additionally to the IRA up to the lesser of $2,000 or 100% of his or her compensation.[5] Therefore, the yearly limit on contributions to an IRA established according to a SEP agreement is $32,000 ($2,000 made by the employee into his or her IRA and $30,000 contributed by the employer).[6] However, if a SEP contribution is made for an employee who is over age 70½, the employee cannot make the $2,000 IRA contribution. Also, that employee must begin taking at least the minimum required amounts of distributions.[7] (See Chapter 3.)

Additional SEP laws prevent discrimination among employees. For example, an employer can base the SEP contribution only on the first $200,000 of each participant's salary.[8] This rule prevents the employer who earns over $200,000 from selecting a contribution percentage that is less than 7½%, but that still allows the employer the full $30,000 contribution. Suppose Mr. Miser owns a successful auto parts store and has a SEP plan. Mr. Miser's salary is $600,000 while all other employees earn $20,000. If Mr. Miser wants to contribute the maximum $30,000 for himself, which is only 5% of his salary, he must contribute at least $1,500, or 7½% of $20,000, for his eligible employees.

Remember that employers, also known as owner-employees, are considered employees in a SEP. A SEP can be established and contributions for a given tax year can be made up to the due date of the employer's tax return, plus extensions. Also, the employer is entitled to a tax deduction for contributions made to the IRAs of its employees.[9]

SEP Effects on Employees

It is important to note how SEP contributions affect employees. If a SEP contribution is made for an individual, he or she becomes an active participant for purposes of the new IRA deduction rules. Recall from Chapter 2 that such active participation status affects the deductibility of regular IRA contributions. Since IRA rules apply once money is contributed to a SEP-IRA, if an employee chooses to withdraw employer-contributed funds soon after the contribution is made, the employee must include that amount as income for that taxable year and pay a 10% premature distribution penalty tax, unless he or she is over age 59½ or is disabled.[10]

An employee also may have income from self-employment. In this case, both a SEP and a Keogh plan are permissible; however, the IRS Model 5305-SEP Plan does not cover this option. A master or prototype plan that permits both a Keogh plan and a SEP would be required. In this case, SEP contribution rules apply to SEPs. Also, in the aggregate, contributions to both the Keogh and the SEP cannot exceed contribution limits of 25% of compensation or $30,000, whichever is less.

Since contributions under a SEP are made to an IRA, the financial institution as trustee is responsible for reporting all contributions and distributions on the proper forms to the individual and the government. (See Chapter 4.)

Leeway Periods

Employers can use a fiscal tax year instead of a calendar year to determine contributions. For most employers who report taxes on a calendar-year basis, this means that a SEP can be established and contributions for a given year can be made up to April 15 of the next year. If the employer files for an extension, the last day a SEP could be established, or on which contributions for the previous tax year could be made, is August 15.

Figure 5-2 compares the leeway periods available for IRAs, SEPs and qualified plans to establish and to make contributions for a given year. As Figure 5-2 shows, an IRA may be opened or continue to accept contributions for a given year up to April 15 of the next year. Extensions past April 15 are not available for IRAs.

SEPs may be opened or accept contributions for a given year up to the date that the employer's tax return is due, including extensions. Also, an employer who uses a fiscal tax year that ends on a date other than December 31 may open or make a SEP contribution for a given year until the due date, including extensions. The due date for nonincorporated employers using a fiscal tax year is three and one-half months after the last day of their fiscal year.

In contrast, qualified plans (e.g., Keogh plans) must be opened by December 31 or the last day of

FIGURE 5-2
Leeway Periods for IRAs, SEPs and Qualified Plans to Open and Contribute for a Given Year

	Establish By	Can Contribute To
IRAs	The following April 15; no extensions	The following April 15; no extensions
SEPs	Due date of employer's tax return, including extensions	Due date of employer's tax return, including extensions
Qualified Plans	December 31 or last day of fiscal year	Due date of employer's tax return, including extensions*

*If established by December 31 or the last day of fiscal year.

the fiscal year used for a given year. If a qualified plan is opened by this date, then it may accept contributions for a given year until the due date, including extensions of its tax return. However, if a business does not establish a qualified plan by its year end, deductions will not be available for that year. This has led some employers to establish SEPs instead of qualified plans.

Integration with Social Security

Integration with Social Security generally means reducing employer contributions to participants by amounts contributed by the employer for the participants under Social Security. This reduces the amount contributed by an employer for the participants because Social Security contributions also are counted for SEP contribution purposes. However, the employer receives only one deduction for Social Security taxes. This means that Social Security contributions that reduce SEP contributions cannot be deducted twice, for both Social Security taxes and as a SEP contribution.

IRS Form 5305-SEP cannot be used if the employer uses integration. But SEP contributions may be integrated with Social Security if an individually developed or prototype SEP agreement is adopted. The laws that permit integration can be found in the Internal Revenue Code under Sections 408(k)(3)(D).

As permitted, an employer may reduce a SEP contribution by multiplying the Old Age Survivors and Disability Insurance (OASDI) tax rate by the participant's compensation, up to the Social Security wage base. The OASDI tax rate, which applies to everyone, does not contain the Medicare portion of the Social Security tax rate. Both the OASDI tax rate and the Social Security wage base may vary from year to year.[11] Figure 5-3 shows the OASDI tax rate for 1987-1990.

The effect of integrating with Social Security allows the employer to make higher percentage-of-

FIGURE 5-3
The OASDI Tax Rates

Year	Rate of Tax
1987	5.7
1988	6.06
1989	6.06
1990	6.2

compensation contributions for participants who earn over a certain salary than for the participants earning less than the certain salary. That certain salary is usually the ceiling amount of wages above which Social Security taxes are no longer taken. For example, in 1986, wages up to $42,000 were subject to Social Security taxes. In 1987, the Social Security taxable wage base increased to $43,800. The employer may choose a rate that is less than the current OASDI rate and compensation that is less than the Social Security taxable wage base, but neither can be greater.

An additional requirement for integrated SEPs may be applicable:
If a self-employed individual employs his or her spouse, there is no reduction in contributions for the spouse. This is because the spouse's wages are not subject to Social Security withholding.[12]

There are a number of methods for integrating a plan which have been approved by the IRS. The following example demonstrates how an integrated SEP plan might work. Suppose the Prime Product Company has an integrated SEP that provides a 15% contribution for all employees. Prime Product has a total of seven employees, including two who are 50% shareholders and officers earning $150,000 each, and five other employees who earn substantially less. The 1987 contribution for each participant is shown in Figure 5-4.

For 1987, the OASDI tax is calculated by multiplying the employee's compensation up to $43,800 by an OASDI tax rate of 5.7%. For the owners, Mrs. Cabinet and Mr. Zendal, employer contributions would be 13.33% of their compensation. For Ms. Martin it would be 9.45% of her compensation. For

FIGURE 5-4
Prime Product Company's 1987 SEP Contributions

Participant	Income	15% Contribution	OASDI Tax	Actual Contribution
Mrs. Cabinet	$150,000	$22,500	– $2,497	$20,003
Mr. Zendal	150,000	22,500	– 2,497	20,003
Ms. Martin	45,000	6,750	– 2,497	4,253
Mr. Roberts	30,000	4,500	– 1,710	2,790
Mrs. Stevens	20,000	3,000	– 1,140	1,860
Mr. Moss	10,000	1,500	– 570	930
Ms. Chattel	10,000	1,500	– 570	930
	$415,000	$62,250	$11,481	$50,769

the remainder of the participants, it would be 9.3% of their compensation.

Because of the Tax Reform Act of 1986, the above advantage of plan integration to employers will be diminished after 1988. Starting in 1989, the rules for integrating SEPs will be changing. Essentially, the new rules will allow a smaller disparity between the percentages which highly compensated employees and nonhighly compensated employees receive.

Salary Deferral SEP

A feature available only to employers who did not have more than 25 employees at any time during the prior taxable year was added to SEPs by the Tax Reform Act of 1986. This feature is known as a salary deferral SEP. A *salary deferral SEP* allows employees to receive cash or a contribution to a

SEP via payroll deductions, if certain conditions are met. Two of the most important conditions are the following:

- The employer did not have more than 25 eligible employees at any time during the prior taxable year; and
- At least 50% of the eligible employees elect to have amounts contributed to the SEP.

Salary deferral SEPs provide employees with the opportunity to tax shelter a larger amount of retirement savings than an IRA, in addition to the amounts contributed into an IRA. The salary deferral SEP follows essentially the same tax rules that govern the very popular 401(k) plans and is also likely to become as popular. However, in order to take advantage of the tax benefits that salary deferral SEPs offer, certain tax laws must be followed.

With a salary deferral SEP, employees can elect to defer a percentage of their salaries—up to a maximum amount of $7,000—from federal income taxes. Some states also allow such contributions to be tax-deferred. Beginning in 1988, this $7,000 cap will be adjusted for inflation.

Employees' contributions are made through payroll deductions. Since payroll deductions have the effect of reducing an employee's take-home pay, salary deferral plans are also known as "salary reduction plans." The amounts contributed are pretax, meaning that they are not reported as income and, therefore, are not subject to federal income tax withholding. However, such elective deferrals are subject to Social Security (FICA) and employer-paid unemployment taxes (FUTA). These deferrals are treated as employer contributions when applying the overall SEP contribution limits of 15% or $30,000, whichever is less. This means that the total aggregate amount of both the employee's elective contributions and the employer's contributions cannot exceed the lesser of 15% of the employee's salary or $30,000.

Another benefit of salary deferral SEPs is that employers can make additional contributions, besides those that the employee has elected to defer, on behalf of the employee. Since the employer-provided contributions may not be conditioned on the employee's elective SEP deferrals, the salary deferral SEP provides employees with two benefits:

- a regular SEP in which the employer makes contributions into the employees' IRAs; and
- the elective deferral feature that provides employees with the opportunity to tax defer some of their income.

In addition to an employee's elective deferrals, he or she can still make additional contributions to his or her regular IRAs, as long as the usual rules for IRA eligibility are followed. Remember that SEP participants are active participants for IRA tax deduction purposes.

Nondiscrimination Rules

Special nondiscrimination rules apply for salary deferral SEPs. These rules prohibit highly compensated employees from electing to defer more than 1.25 times the average deferral percentage (ADP) of all the other eligible employees. A *highly compensated employee* is an employee who at any time during the year or preceding year:

- owned over 5% of the business;
- earned over $75,000 in annual compensation from the employer;
- earned over $50,000 in annual compensation

from the employer and was among the top 20% of employees by pay; or
- was an officer of the employer and earned over $45,000.

For example, suppose the Small Time Company has a salary deferral SEP plan. Small Time has 20 employees, of whom 12 have elected to defer a part of their salaries into the SEP. Also suppose that two of the 12 employees can be classified as highly compensated employees. In this case, the highly compensated employees might want to explain the benefits of a salary deferral SEP to the other employees in hopes of persuading them to participate this plan. Otherwise, the highly compensated employees' elective deferrals will be limited, based on the average percentage that the other employees have elected.

Summary

A simplified employee pension plan (SEP) is essentially an employer plan that is funded by an employer's contributions to employees' IRAs. This plan is an agreement by an employer to fund IRAs for its eligible employees. The Internal Revenue Code Section 408(k) spells out the rules for SEPs.

Under a SEP, contributions for a given calendar year must be made on behalf of every employee who has attained age 21 and has worked for the employer three out of the last five years. However, the employer can exclude employees who earn less than $300 a year, are covered under a collective bargaining agreement and/or are nonresident aliens earning no U.S. income. Of course, the employer may choose age and service requirements that are more lenient, so long as the chosen eligibility requirements apply for everyone.

All employees who meet the SEP's eligibility requirements may use an existing IRA to receive SEP contributions or open IRAs at the financial institution of their choice. Those IRAs are established using the financial institution's usual IRA documentation. For expediency the employee often chooses to open an IRA at the same institution at which the employer has established the SEP. This minimizes the employer's administrative work.

If the employer uses Form 5305-SEP, the employer must give a copy of the completed form to all eligible employees. The employer must also give each participant an annual statement indicating the amount contributed on his or her behalf.

Employer contributions to a SEP become immediately and fully vested for the employee, i.e., 100% vested, meaning the employee cannot forfeit any contributions that were made on his or her behalf.

IRA rules apply once money is contributed to a SEP-IRA. Contributions must be determined under a written allocation formula which specifies two things: the eligibility-to-participate requirements, and how to compute the amounts allocated to employees. The employer cannot discriminate in favor of any employee. However, the employer can change the formula for contributions or eliminate contributions from year to year.

The yearly limit in contributions to an IRA established under a SEP agreement is $32,000 ($2,000 for the employee and $30,000 for the employer). The $30,000 amount will be adjusted for inflation beginning in 1988. A SEP can be established and contributions for a given tax year can be made up to the due date of the employer's tax return, plus extensions. This compares favorably to the time limits imposed on opening and contributing to regular IRAs and qualified plans.

A SEP integrated with Social Security allows employers to count OASDI contributions for employees as SEP contributions. The effect of integrating with Social Security permits the employer to make higher percentage-of-compensation contributions for participants who earn over the Social Security wage base than for those who do not.

A salary deferral SEP allows employees to receive cash or a contribution to a SEP, by payroll deductions, if certain conditions are met. The most important conditions are the following:
- The employer did not have more than 25 eligible employees at any time during the prior taxable year; and
- At least 50% of the eligible employees elected to have amounts contributed to the SEP.

Salary deferral SEPs provide employees with the opportunity to tax shelter a larger amount of retirement savings than an IRA, in addition to the amounts contributed into an IRA. A salary deferral SEP can provide employees with two benefits:
- a regular SEP in which the employer makes contributions into the employees' IRAs; and
- the elective deferral feature that provides employees with the opportunity to tax defer some of their income.

Remember that the total aggregate amount of both the employee's elective contributions and the employer's contributions cannot exceed the lesser of 15% of the employee's salary or $30,000. The employee's elective deferral is limited to $7,000, which will also be adjusted for inflation beginning in 1988. In addition to their elective deferrals, employees can still make contributions to their regular IRAs. However, the employee will be considered an active participant for purposes of the IRA deduction rules.

Special nondiscrimination rules apply for salary deferral SEPs. These rules prohibit highly compensated employees from electing to defer more than 1.25 times the average deferral percentage (ADP) of all other eligible employees.

Finally, remember that the numerous details and regulations regarding IRAs are subject to change. The fact that you have read this book is proof that you are concerned about providing good customer service. To stay abreast of the changes that occur, we suggest you check the latest issue of IRS Publication 590. This publication is available free of charge from your local IRS office. Congratulations, and keep up your good work.

Chapter Questions

1. Explain how an employer may establish a SEP. Also describe the benefits of a SEP to an employer and an employee.
2. Explain whom an employer must cover under a SEP.
3. What information must an employer provide to the employees who are eligible to participate in a SEP?
4. State the contribution limits for SEPs.
5. Explain how an integrated SEP works.
6. Describe the benefits of a salary deferral SEP to an employer and an employee.
7. State the employees' elective deferral limitation for contributions into a salary deferral SEP.

Footnotes

[1] IRC Section 408(k)(2)
[2] Proposed Regulation Section 1.408-7(d)(2); Announcement 80-112
[3] See IRS Notice 81-1 for the type of information which must be given. See also the Department of Labor Regulation 2520.104-49.
[4] IRC 408(k)(3)
[5] IRC §408(j)
[6] IRC §408(j)
[7] IRC §408(a)(6)
[8] IRC §408(k)(3)(C)(i)
[9] IRC §404(h)
[10] IRC §408(d)
[11] IRC §3111(a)
[12] IRC §3121(b)(3)(A)

Glossary

A

accrued benefits The accumulated funds in retirement plans that increase in value as contributions are invested over time.

active participant An individual who is considered by the Internal Revenue Service to be covered by a qualified pension plan. Employers indicate on Form W-2 whether an employee is an active participant. Active participants are eligible to establish IRAs; however, the deductibility of their contributions may be limited.

actual distribution A distribution in which IRA funds are, in fact, received by the participant.

adjusted gross income (AGI) The gross income less the total allowable adjustments for federal income tax purposes. This income includes not only compensation but also interest and investment income and Social Security benefits *minus* certain adjustments (such as moving expenses, Keogh contributions, early withdrawal penalties and alimony). IRA contributions are *not* subtracted in calculating AGI.

after tax The income remaining after federal income taxes have been paid.

allowable contribution A maximum dollar amount a participant can contribute to an IRA for a taxable year. Contributions are deemed allowable if they meet specific rules concerning their composition and timing. The rules governing allowable contributions differ among the various types of IRAs. *See also* excess contribution.

allowable distributions Withdrawals from retirement plans made or begun within a specified time period and following certain guidelines.

Distributions from IRAs before age 59½ are allowed in the case of four exceptions: death, disability, divorce or if payments are taken in the form of annuitized payments. Distributions between ages 59½ and 70½ are allowed in any amount. After age 70½, distributions may be either (a) in full or (b) according to IRS-approved payout schedules.

annuity A contract offered by life insurance companies in which a participant makes regular annual payments, called premiums, for an established time period. Upon the end of the stated time period, called maturity, the insurer provides an annual payment of accumulated benefits to the participant over his or her lifetime. A retirement annuity is one of the three retirement savings programs created by ERISA.

C

compensation Salaries, wages, professional fees and other payments received for personal services actually rendered; sometimes referred to as earned income.

conduit IRA A type of IRA, established with a rollover contribution, that is used to temporarily hold retirement funds being transferred from one qualified pension plan to another.

constructive distribution A type of distribution in which the IRA participant does not receive any IRA funds directly. A constructive distribution occurs when a participant or his or her beneficiary (or other "disqualified person") commits an act which constitutes a prohibited transaction. *See also* prohibited transaction.

contributions The employer and/or employee deposits, deferrals or payments into a retirement plan. *See also* allowable contribution.

contributory IRA A type of Individual Retirement Account established by individuals who set aside all or a portion of their yearly compensation; also called a regular or individual IRA. IRAs are one of three retirement savings programs created by ERISA.

contributory plan A pension plan that allows employee contributions in addition to employer contributions.

curing The method participants use to avoid penalties or to correct actions that might lead the IRS to claim that an excess contribution has been made. *See also* allowable contribution; excess contribution.

D

deductibility An individual's ability to take a tax deduction for IRA contributions.

deduction An item that can be subtracted from taxable income, taxable gifts or the taxable estate, thereby reducing the amount subject to taxation.

disabled The Internal Revenue Code defines a "disabled person" as one who "is unable to engage in any substantial gainful activity by reason of any medically determinable physical or mental impairment which can be expected to result in death or to be of long-continued and indefinite duration."

disclosure statement A nontechnical explanation of all of the IRA rules, terms and conditions that affect the account holder.

distributions A withdrawal from a retirement plan. IRA distributions may be either actual or constructive. An actual distribution is one in which the participant receives payment of the funds. A constructive distribution is any one of several circumstances in which the IRA law deems that the participant has received a distribution, even though the participant has not received payment of any IRA funds. *See also* allowable distributions; lump-sum distribution; premature distribution; prohibited transaction; underdistribution.

E

elective-deferral arrangement A type of SEP. The Tax Reform Act of 1986 made an important tax change relating to SEP agreements affecting small firms (25 employees or less). The Act allows for employees of such small firms to shelter some of their income from taxation by making voluntary contributions under the employer's SEP. *See also* simplified employee pension plan (SEP); salary deferral SEP.

eligibility An individual's ability to qualify for participation in an IRA or qualified plan.

endowment contract A contract offered by life insurance companies that is similar to an annuity. However, the contract provides the participant with a guaranteed sum of insurance, called face value, until maturity. Upon maturity, the value written into the policy, called the principal sum, is paid to the participant.

excess accumulation The difference between the amount that should have been distributed from an IRA and the actual amount distributed. *See also* underdistribution.

excess contribution An amount greater than the

Individual Retirement Account participant's annual allowable contribution. An excess contribution is subject to a 6% penalty imposed on the participant by the Internal Revenue Service. *See also* allowable contribution; curing.

excess distribution IRA distributions made after December 31, 1986, that, in the aggregate, exceed $112,500 during any calendar year. The $112,500 figure is to be adjusted for inflation after 1987. Amounts of excess distributions can be subject to a 15% penalty imposed on the participant by the Internal Revenue Service. This penalty does not apply to distributions over the $112,500 figure pertaining to amounts distributed due to death, a qualified domestic relations order, distributions of nontaxable contributions or amounts that are rolled over within 60 days of distribution.

excess retirement accumulation If at the time of death an individual's interests in qualified retirement plans, tax-sheltered annuities and IRAs exceed the present value of an annuity with annual payments of $112,500 (or the limitation in effect), an excess retirement accumulation results. Excess retirement accumulations can be subject to a 15% penalty tax imposed on an individual's estate by the Internal Revenue Service. The 15% excess retirement accumulation tax is levied against the amount of the present value of the annual annuity payments that exceed $112,500. This is a one-time tax paid by the individual's estate. For example, if a participant with a life expectancy of 10 years dies leaving account balances that would purchase a 10-year annuity of $132,500, the penalty estate tax would be $3,000—15\%$ on the excess, or [($132,500 − 112,500) \times .15$].

F

face value The guaranteed amount of insurance that an endowment contract provides until maturity.

fiduciary A person or corporation with the responsibility of holding or controlling property for another. In this relationship, the institution serves as trustee of the funds deposited by the participant, who is also known as the grantor. The trustee exercises discretionary control or authority over the IRA assets and must meet the legal standards of reasonable care, skill, prudence and diligence in the administration of the IRA funds. For custodial IRAs, the fiduciary relationship is essentially the same as that for trusteed IRAs. *See also* trust account agreement.

fixed rate The term commonly used to describe an investment, such as a certificate of deposit, that pays a constant interest rate until its maturity.

H

highly compensated employee An employee who at any time during the year or preceding year:
- owned over 5% of the business;
- earned over $75,000 in annual compensation from the employer;
- earned over $50,000 in annual compensation from the employer and was among the top 20% of employees by pay; or

- was an officer of the employer and earned over $45,000.

See also salary deferral SEPs.

I

integration with Social Security An Internal Revenue Code-approved method for employers to fund SEP and qualified plan contributions for employees. Integration with Social Security means reducing employer contributions to participants' plans by amounts contributed by the employer for the participants under Social Security. *See also* Old Age Survivors and Disability Insurance (OASDI).

IRA transfer The transfer of IRA funds from one trustee/custodian to another trustee/custodian without any payout of funds to the participant. Because IRA transfers are direct transactions between trustees/custodians, the IRA law views such transfers as separate and distinct from either distributions or rollovers. *See also* rollover; distribution.

K

Keogh plan A tax-deferred, trusteed savings plan that allows self-employed individuals, or those who own their own unincorporated businesses, to accumulate funds for retirement. Employers who establish a Keogh plan for themselves must make the benefit available to qualified employees. *See also* qualified pension plan.

L

leeway period The period of time during which

IRAs may be established or IRA contributions may be made, applying retroactively to the preceding taxable year. The leeway period for IRAs extends to April 15. *See also* taxable year.

lump-sum distribution Withdrawal of an individual's total amount of pension benefits or retirement savings in the form of a single payment or lump sum. All or any part of a lump-sum distribution can be used to make a rollover contribution to an IRA. *See also* distribution; rollover.

M

maturity The end of a stated time period.

N

nondeductible IRA contribution An IRA contribution that may not be deducted from an individual's tax return; however, such contributions are valid in all other respects. Nondeductible contributions pertain to active participants who are above Internal Revenue Code specified income levels. *See also* deduction; active participant; adjusted gross income.

nonforfeitable benefit A benefit that has become vested. An employee's rights to benefits that cannot be lost, regardless of whether or not the employee continues to work for that employer.

O

Old Age Survivors and Disability Insurance (OASDI) The OASDI tax rate, which applies to everyone, is the Social Security tax rate minus the Medicare portion. Both the OASDI tax rate and the Social Security wage base may vary from year to year.

owner-employee An employee who owns a part of the business for which he or she works. Also known as employer.

P

partial distribution rollover A type of rollover that occurs when:
- the distribution is equal to 50% or more of the participant's credit in the plan; and
- the distribution is made for one of the following reasons:
  —death of the participant;
  —disability of the participant; or
  —separation from service (participant retires or leaves employer to take another job).

See also rollover; distribution.

participation The term used to describe the fact that an employee has joined a pension plan.

payout schedule A schedule that lists the dates, frequency and amounts of periodic payments made as distributions from an IRA to the IRA participant.

pension plan An employee retirement program that employers and employees establish and maintain so that they can continue to receive an income after they retire.

period certain A predetermined amount of time during which a participant receives allowable distributions from an IRA. A period certain may be any length of time so long as the period is at least as long as the participant's life expectancy. *See also* allowable distribution.

pledge The act of giving rights of ownership to a lender as security or collateral for a loan. If IRA funds are pledged, the amount pledged is considered a premature distribution no matter what the participant's age and may be subject to a 10% tax penalty imposed by the Internal Revenue Service. *See also* premature distribution.

portability The ability to transfer vested benefits from one retirement plan to another. *See also* vesting.

premature distribution An actual or constructive distribution from an IRA before the participant attains the age of 59½. Premature distributions can be subject to a 10% penalty imposed on the participant by the Internal Revenue Service. *See also* distribution.

premium The price paid for a contract of insurance or for an annuity.

pretax The income before federal income tax.

principal sum The value or amount that is written into an endowment contract policy that is paid upon maturity.

prohibited transaction Any action that results in a constructive distribution from an IRA. The Internal Revenue Service has defined prohibited transactions to cover the following three actions:

- borrowing money from an IRA;
- selling property to an IRA; or
- receiving unreasonable compensation for managing an IRA.

A prohibited transaction can cause the loss of all or part of an IRA's favorable tax treatment. *See also* constructive distribution.

Q

qualified pension plan A classification given by the Internal Revenue Service to a retirement or profit-sharing plan that meets certain requirements; also known as Section 401(a) plan. This classification means only that the plan qualifies for favorable tax treatment.

R

regular IRA *See* contributory IRA.

retirement bond A bond issued by the United States Government as part of an individual retirement savings program, also known as a qualified retirement bond. The retirement bond is one of the three retirement savings programs created by ERISA.

rollover A distribution from a qualified plan or IRA to the participant who subsequently reinvests all or part of the distribution in an IRA. Rollover provisions allow for an uninterrupted tax shelter for the proceeds of a qualified pension plan that are received by an employee due to retirement, separation from a company or termination of a plan. *See also* distribution; lump-sum distribution; partial distribution rollover.

S

salary deferral SEP A type of SEP permitted by the Tax Reform Act of 1986. A salary deferral SEP allows employees to receive cash or a contribution to a SEP via payroll deductions, if certain conditions are met. Two of the most important conditions are the following:
- the employer did not have more than 25 eligible employees at any time during the prior taxable year; and
- at least 50% of the eligible employees elect to have amounts contributed to the SEP.

Also known as an elective-deferral arrangement. *See also* simplified employee pension plan (SEP).

simplified employee pension plan (SEP) An arrangement by which employers make contributions to eligible employee's IRAs. Created by the Revenue Act of 1978, SEPs also are called Section 408(k) IRAs. SEPs are subject to certain nondiscrimination and eligibility requirements.

spousal IRA A type of IRA contribution that enables a working spouse to establish an IRA for his or her nonworking spouse. The Tax Reform Act of 1986 also permits a couple to designate a contribution as spousal even if both spouses have compensation.

T

taxable year The yearly period used as the basis of federal income tax calculations; also known as the tax year. *See also* leeway period.

tax-deferred Having postponed tax liability until a later time. Referring to a tax benefit of IRAs, taxes are paid when IRA distributions are made during a participant's retirement.

tax penalty An additional tax liability imposed by the Internal Revenue Code for certain actions. Congress has enacted penalties to discourage the use of IRAs for other than retirement purposes. These penalties, which are detailed in sections of the Internal Revenue Code, fall into two general categories: loss of tax shelter and specific tax penalties. There are five specific IRS-imposed tax penalties. *See also* excess contribution; premature distribution; underdistribution; excess distribution; excess retirement accumulation.

tax shelter The legal means by which an individual or business reduces or defers tax liability on current earnings.

third-party sponsored IRAs A type of IRA contribution sponsored by an employer, a union, or an employee association; also known as a Section 408(c) IRA.

trust account agreement A contract between the institution, as trustee (or custodian), and the IRA participant as grantor. The trustee is the legal title holder and controller of funds in a trust account established for the benefit of another, according to a trust agreement. The agreement also may name beneficiaries of the IRA trust. Also known as a trust agreement or Form 5305.

trustee The legal title holder and controller of funds in a trust account established for the benefit of another, according to a trust agreement.

U

underdistribution The amount of distributions from an IRA not timely made after the participant attains the age of 70½. Underdistributions can be subject to a 50% excess accumulation penalty imposed on participants by the Internal Revenue Service.

V

variable rate The term commonly used to describe an investment, such as a certificate of deposit, that pays an interest rate that fluctuates during the deposit term according to a predetermined schedule and formula index.

vesting The increase, scheduled in increments, in an owner's rights to the dollar value of a life insurance policy or pension plan accumulation contributed by an employer. Vested benefits also are called nonforfeitable benefits.

Index

A

Accrued benefits, 6
    vesting of, 7
Active participant, 63
Actual distributions, 101–102
Adjusted gross income (AGI), 64–65
Age, and eligibility for IRA contributions, 36–37, 39–40
Allowable distributions, 80–81
    annuitized payments based on life expectancy, 90
    death of participant, 87–89
    disability of participant, 89–90
    divorce of participant, 90
    general rules, 81–82
    minimum distribution incidental benefit requirement, 86
    options for taking, 82–85
    tax treatment of, 91–95
"American Eagle" coins, IRA investments in, 72–73
Annuities, 68
    automatic, 97
    life, 82–83, 151
    qualified, 62–63
    retirement, 73
Annuitized payments based on life expectancy, 90
Automatic annuity, 97

B

Beneficiary
    designation of, 136, 137
        contingent, 136
        primary, 136
    distributions to, 87–89, 160–161
Benefit election form, 152, 153, 154

Benefits, accrued, 6, 7
Bonds, retirement, 11, 25, 73–74

C

Cash property, in IRA distributions, 56
Common law employee, 98, 99
Compensation
    distinction between income and, 38
    and eligibility for IRA contributions, 38–39
    treatment of third-party sponsored
        contributions as, 52
Conduit IRA, 23, 43, 95, 97, 98, 100
Constructive distribution, 102–104
Contributions, 6
    allowable by type, 49–56
    allowable maximums, 45
    deductibility of, 17–18, 62–68
    eligibility for making, 15–17, 34–45
    employee, 6, 8
    excess, 56–62, 105–107
    Federal Deposit Insurance concerns, 48–49
    fully deductible, 64–65
    fully nondeductible, 65–66
    general rules and concerns, 45–49
    monitoring, 149–150
    partially deductible, 66–68
    phase-out, 66–68
    for SEPs, 182–184
    timing requirements, 45–48
    trustees' liability for, 68–69
    types of, 18–24, 35–36
Contributory IRA, 8, 18, 34, 35
    allowable contributions to, 35, 49–50
    creation of rollover IRA from, 44–45
    eligibility for, 11, 39
    leeway period for making contributions,
        46–47, 68–69, 150, 185–186
    retroactive, 47

Credit unions, as IRA sponsor, 70
Custodial account, rollover from to an IRA, 100

D

Death
    and allowable distributions, 86–89
        death after Dec. 31, 1983, 88–89
        death before Dec. 31, 1983, 87–88
    excess distributions after, 106–107
    excess distributions before, 106
Declaration of intention, 152
Deductibility of contributions, 17–18, 62–64
    full deductibility, 64–65
    full nondeductibility, 65–66
    impact of Tax Reform Act of 1986 on, 62
    partial, 66–68
Defined-benefit plan, 63
Disability of IRA participant, allowable contribution on, 89–90
Disclosure statement, 128–129, 130–133
    financial disclosure, 134–136
    regulatory disclosure, 129, 134
Distribution agreement, 152, 154
Distribution forms/procedures, 151–154
Distribution(s), 80
    actual, 101–102
    allowable, 80–95
    to beneficiaries, 160–161
    calculating minimum payment accounts, 154–159
    constructive, 102–104
    excess, 105–107
    lump-sum, 8, 43–44, 81, 151
    options for taking, 82–86, 151
    partial, 44, 81, 97–98
    penalized, 100–107
    pledge of IRA funds, 102
    premature, 101–104

role of financial institutions in making, 150–161
rollovers, 95–100
Distribution statements, 94–95
Divorce of IRA participant, allowable contribution on, 90
Document execution, 121
    deposit information, 136, 138
    designation of beneficiary, 136, 137
    disclosure statement, 128–136
    IRA worksheet, 140–141, 142–143
    optional documentation, 138–144
    plan agreement, 121–127
    signature card, 139–140, 141

E

Earnings, tax-deferred, 5
Economic Recovery Tax Act of 1981, 13, 14
Elective-deferral arrangements, 53–54. *See also* Salary deferral SEPs
Eligibility requirements
    age, 15–16
    compensation, 15, 16–17
    for SEPs, 176–177, 180
Employee
    contributions to pension plans, 6, 8
    eligibility for SEPs, 177, 180
    SEP effects on, 184–185
Employee Retirement Income Security Act of 1974 (ERISA), 10–12, 14, 69
    creation of rollover contributions by, 21
Endowment contract, 73
ERISA. *See* Employee Retirement Income Security Act of 1974
Excess accumulation, 27–28, 104, 105–106
Excess contributions, 56–58, 105–107
    curing, 58–62
    tax penalty on, 27, 56, 58

Excess distributions, 105–106
   after death, 106–107
   before death, 106
   tax treatment of, 27

F

Face value, 73
Federal Deposit Insurance Corporation,
   protection of IRAs under, 48–49
Federal income tax withholding, 93–94, 159–160
Federal Savings and Loan Insurance Corporation,
   protection of IRAs under, 49
Fiduciary, 114
   financial institution as, 114–116
Financial counseling center, 119
Financial disclosure, 134–136
Financial institutions
   annual statements to participants, 165–166
   as IRA sponsor, 70–72
   offering of IRA programs by, 114–118
   optional reports of, 167, 169
   reporting for contributions, 161–162
   reporting for distributions, 162–165
   reporting responsibilities of, 167
   responsibility of, for monitoring IRAs, 68–69
   role of, in retirement planning, 4
Fixed rate, 70
Follow-up programs, 141, 144
Full vesting, 6–7

G

Grantor, 115

I

Income
   distinction between compensation and, 38

types of, 38
Insurance companies, as IRA sponsor, 72
Insurance protection of IRA accounts, 48–49
IRAs
    advantages of, 24
    allowed and barred investments for, 71
    disadvantages of, 24–28
    offering of programs, 114–118
    sponsors, 70–73
    transfers, 21–24, 95
IRA accounts. *See also* Retirement savings plans
    controlling access to, 145–146
    deposit options for, 70–71, 121
    insurance of, 48–49
    opening, 118–144
    servicing and maintaining, 144–169
    terms and conditions for, 117–118
IRA checklist, 147, 148
IRA contributions. *See* Contributions
IRA distributions. *See* Distribution(s)
IRA participant, 18
    annual statements to, 165–166
    introducing IRAs to, 119–120
    reporting responsibilities of, 166–167
IRA plan files, 146–147
IRA worksheet, 140–141, 142–143
IRS Form 941/941-E, 160
IRS Form 1040/1040A, 166, 181
IRS Form 1099R, 162, 163, 164
IRS Form 5305, 116, 122, 124–125
IRS Form 5305-A, 116, 122, 126–127
IRS Form 5305-SEP, 176–177, 178–179, 180–181, 182
IRS Form 5329, 105, 166, 168
IRS Form 5498, 161–162, 165
IRS Form 8109, 160
IRS Form W-2, 64, 181
IRS Form W-2P, 162, 164–165
IRS Form W-4P, 160

K

Keogh Act of 1962, 9-10, 13, 14
Keogh Plan, 9–10, 54, 72
    contributions to, in addition to SEP contribution, 54
    rollover from, to an IRA, 98–99

L

Leeway period, 46–47, 68–69, 150, 185–186
Legal action, role of financial institution in guarding against, 115–116
Legislation, on retirement plans. *See specific acts*
Life annuity, 82–83, 151
Life expectancy, annuitized payments based on, 90
Life expectancy tables, 84
    use of, to calculate minimum payment amounts, 154–159
Lump-sum distribution, 8, 43–44, 83, 151

M

Maturity, 73
Minimum distribution incidental benefit requirement, 81–82, 84, 86
Money market funds, as IRA sponsor, 70
Money purchase plan, 63–64
Mutual fund companies, as IRA sponsor, 72

N

National Credit Union Administration, protection of IRAs under, 49
Noncash property, proceeds from sale of, and establishment of IRA, 24, 55–57
Nondeductible contributions, impact on distributions, 91–93
Nondiscrimination rules, for salary deferral SEPs, 191–192
Nonforfeitable benefits, 6
Notification, 152

P

Partial distribution, 44, 81
    rollover to an IRA, 97–98
Participation, 6
Payout schedule, 82
Penalized distributions, 100–101
    excess distributions, 105–107
    premature, 101–104
    underdistributions, 104–105
Penalties. *See* Tax penalties
Pension plan
    characteristics of, 5–9
    tax treatment of, 9
Pension Reform Act. *See* Employee Retirement Income Security Act of 1974
Period certain, 82, 151
Periodic distribution, 8, 81
Phase-out deductions, 66–68
Plan agreement. *See* Trust account agreement
Pledge of IRA funds, as premature distribution, 102
Portability, 21
Premature distributions, 101
    actual distributions from an IRA, 101–102
    constructive distribution, 102–104
    penalty tax on, 27, 90, 101–104, 184
    pledge of IRA funds, 102
Principal sum, 73
Profit-sharing plan, 63
Prohibited transactions, 103–104

Q

Qualified annuity, 62–63
Qualified plan, 5, 8, 23, 62

R

Regular IRA. *See* Contributory IRA
Regulatory disclosure, 129, 134

Reporting requirements, 161, 171
    annual statements to participants, 165–166, 167
    institution reporting for contributions, 161–162
    institution reporting for distributions, 162–165
    optional institution reports, 167, 169
    participants' reporting responsibilities, 166–167, 168
Required minimum distribution, 83–82, 84, 86
Restrictions, on IRAs, 25
Retirement annuities, 25, 73
Retirement bonds, 11, 25, 73–74
    rollover from, to an IRA, 11, 99, 100
Retirement planning
    advantages of, 5
    major legislation affecting, 9–15. *See also specific acts*
    need for, 4
    role of financial institutions in, 4
Retirement savings plans, 25, 69–70. *See also* IRA accounts
    rollover from one plan to another, 99
Revenue Act of 1978, 14, 20, 55, 105
Revocation, right of, 128
Rollovers, 21–24, 34, 95–96
    age restrictions for, 37
    allowable contributions to, 36, 54–56
    creation of, from contributory IRAs, 44–45
    curing excess contributions for, 61–62
    eligibility rules for, 37, 41–45
    files for, 147
    from Keogh Plan to an IRA, 98–99
    and lump-sum distributions, 43–44
    mix of noncash and cash properties, 56
    noncash distributions, 55–56
    from one retirement savings plan to another, 99

partial distribution, to an IRA, 44, 97–98
from qualified retirement bonds to IRA, 11, 100
sources and placement of funds for, 54–55
from tax-sheltered annuity or custodial account to an IRA, 100
timing of reinvestments, 42
versus transfers, 21–24, 95
Salary deferral SEPs, 189–192. *See also* Elective-deferral arrangements
Savings counselors, role of, in retirement planning, 4–5
Section 408(c) IRA. *See* Third-party sponsored IRAs
Section 408(k) IRA. *See* Simplified Employee Pension Plan (SEP)
Self-directed IRA, 72, 117, 135
    financial disclosure for, 137
    insurance coverage of, 72
Self-Employed Individuals Tax Retirement Act. *See* Keogh Act
SEPs. *See* Simplified employee pension plans (SEPs)
Signature card, 139–140, 141
Simplified employee pension plans (SEPs), 12–13, 20–21, 34, 35–36
    advantages of, 12–13
    age restrictions for, 37
    allowable contributions to, 36, 52–54
    contribution and deduction rules, 182–186
    curing excess contributions for, 61
    elective-deferral arrangements, 53–54
    eligibility rules for, 37, 41, 177, 180
    employer-provided information, 180–182
    establishing, 176–182
    integration with Social Security, 186–189
    making Keogh contribution in addition to, 54

Index

salary deferral, 189–192
Social Security, integration of SEPs with, 189
Spousal IRA, 12, 18–19, 34, 35
    account ownership, 18–19, 51
    age restrictions for, 37
    allowable contributions to, 19, 35, 50–51
    eligibility rules for, 37, 39–40
Stock bonus plan, 63
Stock brokerage firms, as IRA sponsor, 70, 72
Straight amortization method, for calculating distributions, 159

T

Taxable year, 45–46
Tax-deferred rollover contributions, 95–100
Tax Equity and Fiscal Responsibility Act of 1982 (TETRA), 13, 14
    and death of IRA participant, 88
    tax withholding under, 93
Tax penalties, 25–28
    for excess accumulation, 27–28, 104, 105–107
    for excess contributions, 27, 56, 58
    for excess distribution, 27
    for premature distributions, 27, 88, 101–104, 184
    for underdistribution, 27, 104–105
Tax Reform Act of 1976, 12, 14, 18
Tax Reform Act of 1984, 14, 83–84
Tax Reform Act of 1986, 14, 40, 53, 62, 86
    and integration of SEPs with Social Security, 189
    reporting requirements of, 166
Tax shelter, 8
    loss of, for IRAs, 25–26
Tax-sheltered annuity, rollover from to an IRA, 100
Tax treatment, of allowable contributions, 91–95

Technical Corrections Act of 1979, 37
TETRA. *See* Tax Equity and Fiscal Responsibility Act of 1982 (TETRA)
Third-party sponsored IRAs, 19–20, 34, 35–36
    allowable contributions to, 20, 35–36, 51–52
    eligibility rules for, 40–41
    tax status of amounts contributed to, 20
Transfer of rights, from pension plan to pension plan, 21
Transfers versus rollovers, 21–24, 95
Transmatic (R) payment plans, 149
Trust account agreement, 116–117
    execution of, 121–123
    sample, 124–127
    for SEPs, 122, 177
Trustee, 116
    liability of, 68–69

U

Underdistribution, 104–105
    tax treatment of, 27, 104–105
U.S. Retirement Bonds. *See* Retirement bonds

V

Variable rate, 70
Vesting, 6–7
    of accrued benefits, 7

W

Withholding, 93–94, 159–160